WHEN WE WERE YOUNG

INSPIRED BY TALES OF TRUTH, ADVENTURE, LOVE AND LOSS

ROBERT MATTIA

This book is dedicated to my father who made that fateful, courageous journey to lands unknown, and who through his life of hard work, commitment and persistence established a thriving family that went on to become Farmers, Laborers, Builders, Doctors, Lawyers and Proud Citizens.

PREFACE

While reading a book on publishing I became aware that a writer should be motivated by the need to tell a story about what he knows. Other than a thesis in college, my writing has been related to work. I have written numerous articles and publications for magazines and authored many reports during my career as a Project Manager. Then one day I realized I had a story to tell. It was a story that I knew well and wanted to share because it had such a dramatic impact on my family, my life and who I am.

Growing up, I became curious about my parents' lives and their struggles during and after leaving their home behind in Italy. After living through the terror of war in their hometowns, they journeyed across the Atlantic Ocean to start a new life for the same reasons as pilgrims in centuries past. They left to find peace, prosperity, and the ability to send some of their good fortune back home, only to find more hardship and struggle in their chosen country. With time and determination that struggle turned to accomplishment.

I have always loved sharing my parents' stories with

friends and relatives. Initially, I thought these stories were entertaining and interesting pieces of history. The more I shared them the more I felt compelled to write about them. It occurred to me that these treasured memories of my family and my life needed to be recorded before they were lost with the passing of the story tellers. I realized that gathering details and finding a way to effectively share them would bring these stories to life. Rather than focusing on the future, I felt compelled to look back and honor my family legacy with the attention that it deserved.

I have learned that life is a series of notable events held together by a string of forgettable moments. In this book, the focus will be on those notable events. The stories are derived from facts and family folklore. The chronology of those events has been subjected to creativity in order to make the story work seamlessly. As with any recollection of the past, the timing is not always accurately remembered but the memory of the event is typically vivid.

I wanted to share this family history because many of you may have your own stories. They may be embedded in your mind or possibly you have memorialized them in notebooks, scraps of paper or in some computer file. Perhaps this book will motivate you to sit and have that conversation with your mothers, fathers and grandparents and document their stories as well as your own. Do this not just for yourself but for the generations to come who will want to know about the life of their ancestors. My only regret is that I never had the opportunity to record my grandparents' stories.

Our lives are filled with the daily grind to achieve success. We sit at our computers documenting data that someday will become obsolete, storing it in a far-off server possibly never to be retrieved. Memorialize your story. It will live beyond your days and become a part of your family history that will be cherished and read for generations to come. The written word is everlasting and will never fade with time. It will bring clarity to future generations about the past.

Many of you will relate to the events in this book and may remember events long past by reading it. I enjoyed this journey back in time. The walk down memory lane was filled with love, laughter, joy, sorrow, and pain. These are the emotions we must feel and surrender to in order to fully appreciate living and moving forward. I hope you enjoy the time you spend with me in this story inspired by my family.

THE CALL

The day started with little warning of the devastation that would unfold and forever change our lives. The unexpected call would put in motion the final unravelling of my life as I knew it. My family had always been my secure base and slowly over the past four years my safety net had been peeled away one layer after another. It was like I was in a perpetual emotional freefall. Some days were better than others, but always in the very corners of my mind, it was there. Intellectually I knew what was to come. Emotionally I could not have anticipated the unfathomable devastation once it finally arrived. Loss changes us like nothing else. The fallout from the call was something that I never anticipated and at the same time it was something that I knew was coming. The aftermath would forever change my world but in some ways, it did not change my life at all.

It was one of those magnificently beautiful, sunny days that make you feel happy to be alive. As usual, my morning would begin with the alarm clock announcing the start of another routine morning. At precisely six a.m. one of my favorite classic symphonies, Vivaldi's 'The Four Seasons Autumn' came booming from my radio. It jolted me from my peaceful sleep and signaled the start of a day to be filled with the expected humdrum minutia of a working man's weekday life. My predictable morning regimen was about to begin. Awake with the alarm clock. Go downstairs for my daily workout. Next, I would shower and shave, and then get dressed in my usual neatly pressed cotton shirt, tie, and khakis. Afterwards I would brew my Arabica dark roast coffee, grab breakfast and head off to work. I expected this day to bring nothing out of the ordinary. However, it ended up being anything but ordinary.

Normally, I am not one to dwell on the past. My focus is usually on my life as it exists or working to make future aspirations a reality. My mornings are filled with little reflection and much routine approached in a comatose like manner. Monday through Friday mornings are executed in auto mode, but for some reason this day seemed a little different. Not only did the sky seem more brilliant than usual, but my thoughts were equally fine-tuned. My mind was wandering to my childhood and memories were flooding me with each minute that passed, and each routine task performed. With every movement I made, came a vivid memory of my life, my family and what shaped me as a human being.

Even the mild ache in my shoulder and the numb arm I awoke with took me back to memories of my mother. It reminded me of my younger days when I would awaken with one arm completely numb and how it would eventually come back to life with needle like sensations. As a child I would seek comfort and some babying from my mother. But in Mom's typical strong, Italian, maternal way, she would tell me that it was nothing to worry about. The arm had fallen asleep and that the prickles just meant it was coming back to life. She would tell me to be happy that I am alive and that I can feel the prickles.

The first thing I do every morning is done without thought. It is something that was ingrained in me as a child. It cannot even be considered a part of my routine because it is more of a reflex than a deliberate action. When I open my eyes each morning, I do not check my phone. I do not take a shower. I do not eat breakfast. What precedes everything is much more important and vital to a successful day. I make my bed. From the time I was old enough to be aware of anything, the first words I would hear each morning was not wake up, not good morning or what do you want for breakfast. Oh no. Not in my loving, hardworking Italian family. What I heard was my mother bellowing from the kitchen "Non dimenticare di rifare il letto". This incredibly kind, loving woman would suddenly yell like a drill sergeant reminding me "Don't forget to make your bed" as she jolted me out of my sweet young slumber. Motherly platitudes came only after the bed was made.

As a child with OCD tendencies, it was downright scary. I did not dare defy my mother. When it came to bed making it was like she grew another head and became a different person. As a parent, I now realize that she had a job to do and had the confidence in her parenting abilities to enforce it. Now that I am an adult, bed making is still the first thing I instinctively do regardless of where I am in the world.

After the bed was made and I regained control of my arm, I moved on to part two of my morning ritual. I went downstairs to work out in the cold basement. This dungeon-like room was my version of a man cave. Among the antiques, a model ship and artwork I had collected over the years, was a huge television screen which took up a large part of one wall. Across from it sat a family sized sectional sofa. On Sunday and Monday nights, I watched NFL games with friends and drank brown pop, which was adult code for beer in my house.

In another corner sat my home gym where I had a couple of workout mats and weights. After several years of exercise trial and error, I had settled on a routine that started with some stretches, weights, and pushups. The most difficult part of my routine was the 150 crunches I did at the end. People often ask me why anyone would subject themselves to such a brutal regimen. Once again, the answer lies in my childhood.

While delivering newspapers in elementary school I was hit by a car. It did not seem to result in any apparent ill effects during my youth. I was able to join my high school cross country team and we ran for hours along the back roads from one small town to another without any problems. However, as I got older the latent effects came back to haunt me. It left me with a chronic sore back which would send a numbing sensation down my leg whenever I ran or lifted weights. By the time I completed college, it brought my daily running routine to an unhappy end. After attending a sports medicine seminar at a local college, I found that an adherence to a daily regimen of crunches worked and it was then that it became a staple of my daily routine.

When my career brought me from outdoor construction sites into the office, I started to feel sharp spikes of pain shooting through my knees whenever I climbed stairs. The crunches were no longer enough. My daughter Erica, who was by now a chiropractor, told me it was because I sit all day. She prescribed specific leg stretches which helped to alleviate the knee pain. It seemed like the proverbial moment when the child becomes the parent. My daughter was replacing my mother by telling me what I needed to do. The program of combined weights, crunches and stretches were life altering, and being a creature of habit, I still adhere to it every day.

Once my exercise routine was complete, I returned to the bedroom for phase three of my morning. This could only be done after bed-making and exercise. I continued to be consumed with thoughts of my family and what a major influence they were on my life and how I now live. By this time, the gorgeous sunrise was spilling through the half open bedroom blinds illuminating the dark corners of the room. Unfortunately, the shimmering beauty of the sun only highlighted the particles of dust in the air. I noticed that my dresser had accumulated so much dust that I could have planted potatoes in it. This revelation brought me back to reality and reminded me that I had some serious housework to do that weekend.

After a warm shower and basic grooming, I got dressed in my usual button-down shirt and khakis and returned to the kitchen. My Arabica dark roast coffee had finished brewing. As I reached for my customary weekday cherry and dark chocolate granola bar, I thought it was not quite as good as my weekend breakfast of choice – hot oatmeal with chicory powder and a shot of Kahlua – but being a work-day, it would have to do. I filled my travel mug with coffee taking a moment to breathe in that dark rich aroma, grabbed the granola bar and headed to work.

The front door opened to a world of natural splendor. The sun had totally risen by the time I stepped off the front porch. The picture-perfect day filled me with a sense of well-being. The brilliance of the sun overshadowed the sameness that had for so long filled my life. It was going to be a terrific day. I remotely opened the garage door and my truck awaited me. My morning rituals were almost complete. I was ready to move to phase four of my morning. I would usually steel myself for this part of my day, but the thought of my daily treacherous drive to work did not seem as daunting today.

Once I turned on the heater and the seat warmer, I slowly backed out onto the street. The drive took me through picture perfect country roads and past farms with plowed fields. The maple trees were starting to show hints of fall splendor with tiny bits of orange and red blended into the green foliage. This serenity would not last. It was these few moments of tranquility that I enjoyed every morning before I exited to the expressway where the stress of the morning commute would begin. It would be fifteen minutes of racing madness dodging slower drivers on the highway. My peaceful, loving thoughts of morning quickly turned to annoyance and impatience. Don't these people have jobs to get to? Why can't they pick up their speed? Don't they know that driving too slowly is a hazard?

I managed to arrive safely at the massive factory complex where I spent most of my waking hours. I turned my truck into a parking lot that was large enough to accommodate vehicles for a spacious airport facility. However, it was only about thirty percent full. With all the empty spaces you would think that it would be easy to decide on a parking spot. You are wrong. If the spot is too close to the building someone may ding the truck. If it is too far way, someone may vandalize it. Entering the lot, I drove to my usual spot, a spot that felt right. I turned the truck off and headed into work.

Taking a deep breath, I put on my work face and made my way towards the glass styled plant facade. One of our completed projects was to transform the drab front entrance to one that had spectacular modern features with three story high glass and white stone panels. The massive facility was now only a shell of what it once was when it housed about 2,500 employees. Severe downsizing of the workforce had taken place not only due to changing market conditions, but due to repurposing part of the plant from a foundry into an engine assembly operation. This left a workforce of only 800 people. Automation had improved production, but it had decimated the jobs and adjusted people's lives.

Once inside, the serenity of my morning was replaced with the familiar sounds of machines humming and people chatting. I swiped my security card, went through the turnstile, and headed past the security window. Going up a flight of stairs, I greeted coworkers along the way. Since it was the start of the production shift change, the morning workforce was intermingled with the people that I routinely work with. Many of the employees leaving were people that I had worked with on previous projects when we revamped and upgraded the production lines. It felt nice to cross paths with former associates that I was familiar with but did not regularly see. Everyone moved with a sense of urgency intent on either getting to their workstation or getting home.

Once I arrived at my desk and engaged in the regular morning banter with my staff, I reached for my day timer. My life related to work was spelled out in that book. My hand scratched priorities helped me organize my thoughts and movements for each day. I glanced down at the list that I had made the previous evening. A quick phone call was made to confirm these priorities with Dave, my project sponsor and owner representative. I loved working with Dave. He was a longtime employee and a well-respected authority in the organization. We got along well and he was someone I could always count on. I was the Contract Project Manager responsible for getting this massive $450,000,000.00 project completed on time and on budget. We were revamping almost half the plant from an old metal foundry to a new engine assembly line. The construction revamp involved jack hammering concrete floors, replacing massive concrete slabs, and installing miles of machines, pipes, and electrical cables. Dave was tasked with making sure the job was completed as required. There were half a dozen contractors on site to make it happen. We both felt that transparency was the key to our combined success.

After our short conversation, I was off to the operating floor for the daily morning huddle. This gathering of the project decision makers was held inside the construction barriers every day of the many months long upgrade. These huddles, widely attended by Engineers, Coordinators and Contractors helped incentivize the work force and provide some guidance. For about fifteen minutes each morning, this group of focused stakeholders would gather so we could go over the day's plans and looming deadlines. We discussed routine housekeeping items that involved priorities, delays, and safety issues that we would encounter that very day. At the conclusion of the meeting there were usually side bar discussions taking place between parties who needed to make further coordination efforts. The meeting was memorialized by felt pen markings on a white board where I would list the top tasks for that day. It was just another routine day on the job performing routine tasks.

Outside our walled-in construction project area, the plant had a half dozen production lines operating at full capacity and it was imperative that our work did not impede on their operations. If we inadvertently shut down a line for any reason, top ranking personnel including myself would be hauled into the plant manager's office for an unpleasant dress down. No one wanted that. Any tie into existing operations had to be planned with excruciating detail. Timing was critical and any shutdown needed to be communicated with a wide range of stakeholders. Full details of shutdown operations were studied and mutually agreed to by all affected parties.

These numerous shutdowns to tie into existing systems could take from one hour to full shifts and were planned for lunch hours, shift changes or holiday production shutdowns. When everyone was at home enjoying the holidays with their families, we were working feverishly around the clock making needed changes and adjustments in the plant. As the client's Project Manager, my company was contracted to ensure the timely installation of a state-of-the-art engine manufacturing facility. Leading a Project Management division within the corporation, I also needed to occasionally keep tabs on other projects. The job was demanding and could be stressful at times. It was imperative that I always keep a cool and clear head.

On this particular day it seemed like we were on track for an on-time completion which would leave the customer happy and provide us with additional opportunities. These engines had to be ready for installation into the chassis of new model year vehicles at another plant. They were gearing up to receive them on a specific date. No one wanted to be the bad guy and miss their target date. Unknown to us at that time, competition was heating up and market conditions would dictate that the client shave another three months off an already tight schedule.

As I headed back to my office, I made my way through lines of running machinery. The office was located in a forty by eight-foot-wide job trailer consisting of plywood and white sheet metal siding sitting on load jacks. The interior was decorated with cheap wood paneling and filled with used desks, chairs, tables and filing cabinets. It was positioned inside the massive 1,000,000 square foot facility but separated in a corner far from plant operations. This was the center of my weekday life. My attention to detail and the structure that my mother drilled into me as a child came into play at my workplace. In some ways she was responsible for my on-the-job success.

As I moved through the plant, I thought of how much I enjoyed the past weekend and my surprise forty-fifth birthday party. I managed to live to see the year 2001. The thought brought me back to my younger years and how I always wondered if I would ever live long enough to see the turn of a new century. Back then, I thought reaching the new millennium would be a major milestone. The movie, *2001 A Space Odyssey*, had left us with a futuristic image of what lay ahead. The cartoon, *The Jetsons* made us believe that flying cars and vacations on the moon awaited us in the future.

I had also read the book *Future Shock* by Alvin Toffler. Back in the 1970s it had quite an impact on me. Toffler was quite insightful and many of his futuristic predictions have come to be realized. In fact, the one prediction that really caught my attention was that we would all have a unique number and that we could be contacted anywhere in the world with that number. He had visualized mobile phones long before their inception. He also predicted interchangeable families for Project Managers as they travelled the globe to remote projects. Admittedly, that concept was a bit out there. As a young kid growing up in a small farming town, what was predicted for the year 2000 seemed unfathomable.

As I continued my way past operating machines and

assembly lines, the sound of machinery humming and chain belts clicking surrounded me. The faint smell of oil filled the air. As I rounded a corner, I almost tripped over a production worker sitting on the floor listening intently to a radio he was holding in his hands.

As I approached him, he looked up at me, shook his head and said with a look of horror on his face, "The third world war has just begun!" I recognized the man from past contacts and previous projects in the plant.

I stopped and looked at him and asked, "What's up Steve?"

He looked at me with piercing eyes and said, "We are in a world war."

He turned up the volume on his radio and it became clear to me that today's events were not going to be typical anymore. As I listened to the broadcast, I could feel a chill run up my back. Horrified, I moved away.

Walking with a sense of purpose, I made my way into my office trailer. As my staff worked diligently at their computers, I asked "Did any of you hear what's going on?"

They looked up from their work and stared at me with emotionless faces.

I said, "Turn on the radio."

"What's happening?" asked my assistant Cari. She approached the radio and turned it on.

We sat together and listened. Our astonishment gradually turned to fear and anxiety. The mood in the room had changed. We were incredulous. A routine, predictable day had somehow turned into a day of chaos and uncertainty. How could this be happening? We were gripped by the moment to moment unfolding events that were reported repeatedly by the media. I could sense the dismay, anxiety, and sheer terror amongst my coworkers. We were mesmer-

ized by the unbelievable events and spent the better part of
an hour listening intently. Eventually we went back to our
desks and tried to focus on the work at hand, but we kept
the radio on for the rest of the day to stay informed. This
day that had started with such beauty and loving thoughts
of days past had just turned into visions of horror and
carnage.

That evening's television coverage was filled with more
of the same. Unforgettable images of the twin towers
collapsing were played repeatedly. Every channel was filled
with carnage, mayhem, and death. We were numbed with
horror, but we could not tear our eyes away. Tuesday,
September 11th, 2001 would go down in history as a
defining moment in our lives much like the assassination of
JFK and the space shuttle Challenger disaster. Years later,
the events of this day are still permanently implanted in our
minds, never to be forgotten.

The next morning, conversations were centered on the
previous day's life altering developments. It was unfathomable that planes could take down the World Trade
Center in New York City. Emotionally we felt this could only
happen somewhere else in the world, in a country already
ripped apart by war. Logically, as construction workers, we
understood the structure of high-rise buildings and were
amazed at how easily they came down. The loss of life
weighed heavily on us as we tried to imagine the terror of
being trapped in a burning building that was about to crumble. I knew that thoughts of work would be secondary to
what was happening in New York City, Washington D.C.,
and Pennsylvania. Work expectations became secondary to
dealing with trauma and fear. Most conversations were
centered on September 11th. Much of the day was spent
reassuring and supporting one another even though the

consolers felt as off kilter as the people they were trying to console.

Still in shock, I scheduled a work meeting for later that afternoon. We had to somehow stay on schedule. My flip phone rang, and I saw that it was my mother. I took a second look just to be sure. She never called me during work hours. In fact, she hardly ever called me at all. It was my duty as her first-born Italian son to call her every Sunday and I always obliged. Obviously, whatever it was could not wait until then. Perhaps she was frightened by the events in New York and needed to talk about it. Having lived through World War II, maybe she was worried that world conflict was imminent.

My parents lived about two hundred miles away from me in a small, sleepy, lakeside farming and factory town with approximately 10,000 residents. It was your typical four corner place sporting a small Carnegie library with a population mostly of German, Dutch and Italian origin. Many of the current townsfolk immigrated there to start a new life after the First and Second World Wars. They came as laborers working on farms and in factories earning meager wages. Daily struggle was a way of life. They were housed in compounds and shacks and often worked seven days a week. Eventually many of these immigrants were able to save enough money to buy property and start their own small farms or gain better jobs at the processing plant that took in all the farm produce. Was my mother calling about the World Trade Center or was it something else?

I pressed the button with anticipation and answered, "Hi Mom, what's up?"

My mother, replied, "Bobby!" She always called me by my childhood name.

In her broken Italian English she said, "You need to

come here and have a talk with your father." Conversations over the phone with my mother were typically short. She always worried about the cost of long-distance charges and never liked to discuss personal matters on the phone.

"Ok Mom. Is everything alright?" I asked

She responded in a phrase I'd heard many times before, "You'll find out. Your father wants to talk to you."

My curiosity was peaked. "What's going on? Does it have to do with the plane crashes?"

In her thick Italian accent, I heard, "You'll find out. Venire." Venire means come in Italian.

I knew my mother and I knew there was no way she was going to give me even a hint over the phone as to what was going on.

"Mom, it's Wednesday. Do I need to come right now?"

"No. Tu lavori. Then you come," she replied.

I ended the conversation with, "I'll be there this Saturday. Tell Dad. Ciao Momma."

My mother, like many immigrants of that time, never perfected her English. Our typical dinner conversation would consist of my mother speaking Italian, my father speaking Italian and English, and my siblings and I would reply in English. She understood English quite well but could not speak it fluently. My siblings and I could understand her Italian, but we were not fluent in the language. The only phrase my mother perfected was "I no speak da hinglish". She selectively used this phrase whenever an unsolicited salesman came to the door trying to sell her something that she did not want or need. There were times when she would attempt to speak completely in English but it would typically be mixed together with Italian. Not only did it make for interesting conversation, but it also helped me develop some Italian speaking skills. It seemed perfectly normal to me.

I smiled recalling a time when we were all gathered in the living room on Christmas Day in front of the silver tinsel tree with the tri-colored rotating flood lights. We were talking about imaginary characters. Mom found it difficult to identify things by name in English so she would embark on a description that would help identify what she was referring to. On this occasion she tried to describe a unicorn. Not knowing the proper name, she described the animal as a horny horse. Once we finally got the connection, we all burst into uncontrollable laughter. Every so often Mom was good for a "ridere" or laugh with her renditions. Of course, she would laugh along with us. We never belittled her attempts; it was always in good fun. Luckily, my mother had a terrific sense of humor. My father, however, spoke English very well and managed to avoid any peculiar descriptions or comical pronunciations except for one. He would say 'hass' as in don't fall on your hass.

In the Italian culture, discussions of family affairs or serious matters did not happen when the kids were around. As young children we understood that matters of the home stayed in the home. It was like we lived in a private society sworn to secrecy. Years later, after my first marriage ended, my parents concealed the breakup for months before telling the rest of the family. Embarrassment was something no Italian family wanted. It was not until we grew up that this code of silence started to fall apart to some degree.

The call from my mother was on my mind the rest of the day. I was trying to rein in my imagination, trying not to worry about what I might find back in the old town. At this point, we had been struggling with my father's slowly progressing debilitating illness for years. I had just seen him recently and he did not seem any better or any worse than usual. With that phone call, I did not realize that my world was about to be turned upside down. What I was about to face was far more difficult to manage and deal with than a daily workplace huddle. I was about to embark on one of the most challenging periods of my life.

2

THE LITTLE OLD TOWN

I was born into a first-generation Italian immigrant family in the 1950s and lived in my hometown until I left for college. Everything I learned about life, love, respect, and hard work I learned in this little town. At the time I thought that everyone lived as we did. I was not aware of generational poverty. War was something that happened in faraway countries. We lived a sheltered, cloistered existence and I did not realize or appreciate until I was much older how incredibly fortunate I was to grow up in this quiet, uneventful town surrounded by a large extended Italian family. It was only after I moved away and had children of my own that I began to grasp what a unique time and place I grew up in.

The town's roots date back to the late 1800s when it was predominantly a lumber town. Over the years, agriculture slowly overtook lumber and it remains the main industry. I grew up on Martin Drive, a street with a slight grade and many Italian families. Unremarkably, I was related to most of them. We were known as WOPs. The belief is that the term originated on Ellis Island during the great migration at the turn of the century. When Italians arrived with little or no documents the immigration agents would place W.O.P. on their entry forms as an acronym for the words 'Without Papers'. As a child I never understood the meaning of the term. I just knew that it did not feel good when kids called me a WOP and laughed.

The term also could have been derived from the Italian term 'guappo' which described a dandy or laborer. It was later shortened to 'guapp' and then with a little English it became WOP. The term evolved into a commonly used derogatory description of Italians. WOP and 'grease ball' or "Degoe" were every day, widely accepted insults hurled at me during my childhood. Cultural sensitivity was pretty much nonexistent at the time. In today's world, WOP is a rarely heard slur. The only exception would be when some of us WOPs use the word as a term of endearment towards one another. No one outside of our culture should dare to use it.

During the 1960s, when every small-town kid just wanted to blend in, it was not easy for me to hide my Italian heritage. My shiny, wavy jet-black hair and European features usually gave me away. I also had a 'unibrow', which my mother said gave me devil eyes. My Roman nose with a small bump on the bridge did not help. The bump I cannot blame on heredity. It was the result of a nasty nose and bed frame collision while jumping up and down on the bed. The large nose in relation to my small child's face protruded beyond what a normal ski hill slope should look like. There was no way to conceal this behemoth nose. Through their teasing and name calling, the kids at school made it clear that this was my defining feature. I tried to deal with the insults when my 'friends' would tease me because of my appearance and ethnicity. Usually, I would return the favor by calling them whatever appropriate slur I could think of, all in the spirit of comradery. Thankfully, as I grew older, my head size increased and my proboscis appeared less dominant. I like to think that the ribbing I got during my childhood gave me a thick skin and developed my strong coping capabilities.

As young kids we spent many hours building push carts out of scraps of wood and lawnmower parts. These rudimentary machines were a flat piece of board with an attached wooden seat, a backboard, an axle and four wheels. A number or name would be painted on the backboard. The wheels came from old lawnmowers or wagons. They did not have to match. They just had to be round and available. Steering was a rope tied to each side of a front wooden board that swiveled with the makeshift axle we nailed to it. We used discarded rusty concrete rebar found at new home construction sites for the axle. If we were not lucky enough to find U shaped nails to attach the axle to the board, we bent straight nails and made them fit. However, these would eventually give out and leave you in the dust on race day. We became miniature machinists and carpenters raiding our fathers' toolboxes for bolts, nuts, and washers. We cut, nailed, drilled, and hacksawed the endless hours away as we built our dream machines.

Each team would show off their work and we would then race these speed machines down the street two or three at a time. Even though they were very primitive pieces of technology these carts satisfied our competitive natures and filled our days. The key element to a successful run was a driver with nerves of steel and a pusher with both stamina and a strong cut hockey stick. It was always best to have the fastest kid on the street as your pusher, so some form of bribery was usually needed for recruiting. Once the cart and the crew were ready to go, we would organize drag race contests with kids from other neighborhoods. The coveted trophies I fashioned from bits and pieces of wood and toy cars. The winner's certificate was hand drawn on any type of blank paper we could find.

One of the sleekest carts was owned by a boy named Todd who lived at the uppermost part of the street. His dad made him one of the best push carts we had ever seen. It had a chassis and a body made of thin, curved plywood. It sat low to the ground, and you could sit inside the cart and only have your helmeted head protrude. We would race these custom-built carts down the dead-end street for about one hundred yards. On one legendary race day, Todd's cart became the center of attention. Todd and his pusher were heading for victory when for some unknown reason he lost control and veered off course. Instead of heading to victory, he headed directly under a parked stake truck. He slammed into the back of the vehicle with a thud, and the cart with Todd still in the driver's seat disappeared underneath. After it was over, and the shock subsided, we all ran to help him fearing the worst. We were sure that this poor kid was going to be decapitated when we pulled him out.

Luckily, he was just unconscious, still sitting in his cart with his head intact. Had it been one of our flat board carts he would have been a goner. He had the wind knocked out of him, so we collectively dragged him and the cart out from under the truck, carried him to the grass and laid him down. We just stood and watched for a sign of life. No one thought to run for help. All of a sudden, he gasped for air and let out a full breath. He was alive. He immediately sat up and started to cry when his dad arrived. His father was angry but happy to see that his son was relatively okay. Poor Todd's racing days were over. Soon after the accident, his father dismantled the cart and he was relegated to spectator status.

He never raced again. Many years later these wooden push carts would be replaced with low riding, steel framed motorized go carts sold in stores. Although they outperformed our workmanship, I still think fondly of our homemade creations and the hours of entertainment they gave us.

My love of cars, especially race cars or custom rods came from these basic homemade vehicles. It was also the beginning of my love of art and drawing. I developed a talent for sketching sports cars and custom cars. My friends would ask me to draw their favorite hot rod so they could hang it on their bedroom wall or glue it to their binder. I spent hours drawing, coloring and even designing newly imagined vehicles for friends.

It was around this time that skate boards arrived on the scene. Using our acquired cart building skills, we would disassemble old steel roller skates and attach the wheels to the underside of an elliptical wooden board we cut out of a piece of wood. With the slope on our street many hours of skate boarding entertained us during long summer days.

With the arrival of winter, the cold, bitter weather would dump massive amounts of snow and would temporarily put an end to our car racing endeavors. This is when we honed our survival skills and created snow forts where we would marvel at our workmanship and huddle together for warmth. The snowy weather also brought out the sleds, toboggans, and metal disks. We would go down the snow-covered slopes howling, sometimes with four or five of us on one toboggan. The best hill was a steep slope near the town line next to the local cemetery. Here you had to stop yourself by falling to one side. If you did not, you risked hitting a tree or landing in a pond of water. The bigger the risk, the more exciting the run.

The ice that formed in the flooded fields surrounding

our neighborhood prompted many friendly games of pickup hockey. After clearing the snow, we used handmade hockey sticks and old ratty pads. The stick was usually rendered useless after a good slap shot if your assembly skills were substandard. The blade which was attached to the stick with black hockey tape would dangle like a broken arm. If you skated too far to the edge of the ice you risked falling through into a pocket of water. If you were the unlucky one, you had to go home as quickly as possible before your pants froze up and left you walking like a stick man, stiff and cold.

When we had a winter thaw, water would accumulate at the base of the sloped street and freeze overnight leaving a sheet of ice. Uncle Chip, as we called him, lived directly across from that patch of ice. He would flood the ice each night to give it a nice smooth top coating. He was a neighbor who could be counted on to always inject some joy and excitement into our day. We loved the man because he would take the time to build or create projects for us. In today's world, the time he devoted to us kids could mistakenly be viewed as suspicious, but he was genuine. There were no sketchy situations with Uncle Chip. He understood his boundaries and was well known and respected by everyone on the street. Today he would be known as a sanitary engineer. In the 1950s and 1960s, he was known as the town's garbage man.

As a young child I would often sit on the cold curb watching with envy as the neighborhood children skated in circles and slapped pucks around. Initially, I could not join in because I didn't own a pair of skates. Like everyone else in those days, we were all quite poor and most parents did not have money for much beyond food and shelter. Clothes were functional hand me downs that were traded back and forth with other relatives. My struggling parents could not afford to buy me skates like the other kids had. This left me watching and wishing. My guess is that Uncle Chip saw me sitting on the sidelines and realized why. One day he approached me with an old pair of worn out black and brown leather ice skates with a bit of rust on the blades. As a garbage collector, he had access to many discarded but still usable items, and I suspect that is how he acquired the skates.

Uncle Chip approached me with the skates and said, "Here. Try these on."

I replied, "Wow! This is for me? Thanks, Uncle Chip." They were well used but they were brand new to me. With some thick socks to fill the extra space in the toes I managed to wobble about on the ice with the other kids and hone my skating skills. I now felt like I belonged and was just like everyone else.

Those were innocent times. We played hide and seek or monopoly late into the night. From the spring through the fall, the boys played baseball in a farmer's dusty field. The girls would play with their Barbie dolls, pushing little baby carriages or cooking with their play kitchens. We were still years away from gender equality.

Once spring arrived, our obsession was road hockey. The game would immediately stop when someone would yell 'car' and we would move the nets off the street and out of the way. Once the car passed the game would resume without skipping a beat until the next car tried to pass by. On any given day, we did this numerous times, over and over again. It was a part of the game and did not hamper the fun that we had.

A summer activity that was almost as exciting as road hockey was a rousing tomato fight. Prior to any uprising we would pick sides and hunker into selected rows in the tomato field. We would then wage our rendition of civil war. The losing team was the one with the bloodiest looking tomato stains on their clothes. Luckily, the farmer's house was well out of eyeshot and he was oblivious to what we were doing.

If we were not throwing tomatoes, we would sit and eat them in the field. To enhance the flavor, we would come equipped with a saltshaker and half a loaf of bread. We would feast until we could eat no more. To this day, it is difficult to find a tomato that comes close to the taste of those we picked right from the field. Today's greenhouse grown varieties or those with genetic modifications just do not taste like a real tomato to me.

At harvest time, the farmers would hire pickers to load the tomatoes into tall, conical, wire rimmed wooden baskets. They would then carefully stack them four to six rows high on wagons which were hitched behind tractors. The loaded wagons looked like red pyramids being pulled through the streets. They would head to the factory in town for processing into tomato soup, sauce, or ketchup. Occasionally, a wagon would hit a pothole and some of those baskets would fall and leave piles of smashed tomatoes strewn all over the now red stained street. Even the damaged tomatoes littering the street would provide our young minds with an opportunity for entertainment. As soon as we heard the news of a spill, we would run to the scene and grab the spoils. We would then lay in wait to bombard semi-truck trailers with the tomatoes as they passed by. In the winter months we had to regroup and use snowballs to continue our assault on passing trucks.

My father, who worked at the plant, would tell me how these tomatoes would be loaded onto conveyor belts before being washed. On either side of these rolling conveyor belts, women had to pick out the spoiled tomatoes, rocks, and twigs. It was common to hear a shriek as an occasional frog or snake rolled by mixed in with the tomatoes. My father said that these episodes would inject laughter into an otherwise boring day.

In the springtime, at the start of the growing season, there were nights when the local farmers would haul dump truck loads of fresh horse and cow manure mixed with straw. They would have these loads deposited throughout their fields in piles up to ten feet high. This was the standard before fertilizer was widely used. On most nights, the distant sound of the lonely train whistle lulled you to sleep. On these nights, if the breeze was not coming from the right direction bedtime would not be so pleasant. Your sleep would be transformed into a long and restless night filled with the wafting smell of manure that permeated the air. Without air conditioning, the windows had to stay open on warm nights or it would be too hot to sleep upstairs. Back then, air conditioners were non-existent. The only cooling method was an electric fan you could stick your finger into set in an open window. Unfortunately, it only moved the smelly air around. You had a choice to make. You either sucked up the smelly air or closed the window and sweat all night. With either choice, sleep was minimal.

After sitting in the sun for a few days, the manure piles would develop a nice hard crust concealing the biohazard mash just underneath the surface. A friendly competition of 'King of The Castle' would then be the game of the day. The object was to be the first one to get to the top of the dung pile without breaking through the dry hardened shell. Failure meant filling your shoes with the pungent excrement. Needless to say, our moms were not thrilled when we walked through the door at the end of the day. I am not sure if we did not know any better or if it was so much fun we did not care. So, we had a bit of cow poop on our clothes. Oh well. Remarkably, no one ever got sick or died from it. Eventually the farmer would load the manure into his spreader and fling it everywhere. We would then have to use our imaginations to create a new game somewhere else.

To cool off during the summer months, we would go to the community public pool. It was there that I experienced my first death defying water event. Why is it that when we are young, we try so hard to fit in even if it means possible death? On one particularly warm summer day, I decided to go to the pool with a group of friends. I feared water and had never learned to swim. My day would be spent sitting at the shallow end of the pool while my buddies did swan dives off the diving board. I was so envious of them. It did not look too difficult, but my fear kept me at the shallow end.

As usual, my friends called out and asked me to join them on the diving board. They had no idea I could not swim. I usually declined the request, but on this day, I left the shallow end of the pool and headed to the diving board. It was embarrassing to sit on the edge of the pool by myself. My heart pounded in my chest as my nervous tension grew. I stood in line for the diving board and watched anxiously as each kid took his turn. As the line got shorter and shorter my anxiety increased to a fever pitch. It was now my turn and I slowly walked to the end like a doomed pirate on Black Beard's ship. I held my breath, looked at the water below and jumped. Crazy as it sounds, I thought that somehow, I would miraculously be able to swim once I jumped in. Unfortunately, that did not happen. Panic set in and I was completely disoriented and thrashing about. I thought this would be how my life ends. Thankfully, out of nowhere, I felt an arm around my neck. I was being pulled to the shallow end where my feet could touch the bottom of the pool. Standing up, I wiped the water from my face and looked directly into the lifeguard's eyes. I told her I did not think the water was that deep.

She gave me a stern look and said, "You stay in the shallow end."

"Yes ma'am," I replied. Relieved to be alive, I happily complied. Except for the embarrassing fact that a girl saved my life, I knew it was my lucky day. The only downside was that all my friends now knew that I could not swim. My buddies found it hilarious. It was many years before I could go to the pool and not expect merciless teasing. Thankfully, this happened at a public facility with a lifeguard on duty and not at the farm irrigation pond where we often went to cool off.

During the winter, our attention shifted from the pool to the aging town arena next door. Swimming at the public pool would be replaced by minor league hockey and public skating. On a cold January day, armed with mittens, warm clothes and a pair of skates my father dropped me off at the arena. I waved as he drove away. As I laced up my skates a rumor started to make its way around the arena. Apparently, there was a train derailment just down the road. I did not give it much thought until my father picked me up two hours later.

On our way home we stopped to check out the train wreck. This was big news in our little town. Nothing much out of the ordinary ever happened. There, stacked like cords of wood were approximately twenty-five box cars strewn about and jammed between the warehouse and the old train station. My father said there were no injuries but there was obviously plenty of damage. That is when he told me that he was the third car in line at the rail crossing when it derailed. He was waiting for the train to go by when he heard the loud squeal of metal friction and then a crashing sound. He watched as box cars flipped and tumbled onto one another. It was sheer luck that the cars did not derail where my father had stopped. The boxcars at the crossing were off the tracks but were still standing upright. In hindsight I realize how lucky my father was to be alive. At the time I just thought it was so cool that he saw it happen. I wished that I could have been with him.

The people in my little town were tightknit and connected. There was a sense of stability, peace, and togetherness. Occasionally this sense of security would be shattered by the wailing emergency sirens that had to be tested every few months. We were in the grips of a cold war and had to be ready for an enemy attack at any moment. In school, the 'hunker down under our desk' procedure had to be practiced. It was an ominous reminder that not all was well in the world beyond the simple, innocent lives we led in our little postage stamp town.

A strong sense of community also played a leading role in our safety. Parents knew all the kids on the street and kept one another updated on the actions and whereabouts of their offspring. It was networking delivered by dial up landline phones and word of mouth rather than fiber optics and the internet. Long before prosperity and innovation turned our social circles into a random collection of names and photos we stayed connected in this most simple way.

Looking back at my childhood, I realize that we have lost some of the basic human values and connections of the past. It feels like we are sometimes too busy struggling to become successful to take the time to care about and pay attention to others. Brief printed messages have replaced a phone call and the sound of another human voice. The people that we are sometimes closest to are unknown strangers hiding behind a computer screen. In today's world, it seems the more that we are connected, the more we are disconnected. The world that surrounded my life on Martin Drive was filled with turmoil and unrest, and yet it was still an age of innocence and idealism. It was a time long before the pace of life accelerated, technology advanced and human contact was not human or actual contact at all. It was a blessing to grow up surrounded by my large Italian family in my little town.

3

MARTIN DRIVE

Our first house was on Martin Drive, a turn of the century neighborhood on a dead-end street. The homes were surrounded by farmland that rotated crops of corn, tobacco, and tomatoes. Each week a small van would pull up and an old man would appear to sharpen knives, saws or skates. The house was an old-oversized structure covered in grey particle siding which may or may not have contained asbestos. On the outside, the only features it boasted were a front and back door and a few windows. This drab house did not appear to be a dream home, but it was a dream finally realized for my hardworking-immigrant parents.

Inside, the décor was dated even by 1950s standards. Except for the shiny yellow tiles that covered the bathroom, the walls were painted either dark green or red. The kitchen had flimsy makeshift cupboards with plywood doors that were painted white, and a floor covered with twelve-by-twelve-inch alternating green and red linoleum tiles. Light brown thread bare shag carpet covered the living room floor where the only furniture was a couch, a television, and a bookcase. Inside the bookcase was a set of encyclopedias that my father had bought from a door-to-door salesman. As the years passed Dad would make improvements to the stark appearance of the property by adding a willow tree, shrubs, and a couple of porches. He lined the back perimeter of the yard with evergreen trees in an effort to block an open farmer's field.

The house was about 1,200 square feet in size and had one hundred feet of frontage to the street. A latched door in the bathroom led to a frightfully dark, dingy, smelly basement. One half was still a crawl space with a dirt floor. The other half was a cramped area with a concrete floor and block walls. After a torrential rainfall, the basement would fill with water almost to the top of the stairs. I remember once seeing a timber post floating by when I opened the door. If a heavy rainfall was expected, my father knew he would have to leave work early to save us from drifting away.

Our house held many religious artifacts. Crosses, figurines, and rosaries were standard in a Catholic Italian home. We never managed to obtain the popular bathtub Virgin Mary monument, but we did have several of the Patron Saints gracing our home. There were too many for me to remember. A glossy portrait of the Virgin Mary pasted to a slab of cut wood still encircled with bark was a focal point in the living room. Hung from that picture was the prerequisite rosary with black beads and a crucifix. Without knowing the significance of this plaque, I often used it as a dart board. To this day it hangs in my mother's home with pitted holes all over it. At the time, my parents were furious. As a young boy, I was sure that I was doomed to hell. Today, I am guessing that it is a fond memory of me as a child.

That was where I lived, grew, and built memories for the

better part of my early life. My parents were proud of this old, rundown house they had been able to buy. It was not fit for a king, but they felt like royalty having a house to call their own in their newly chosen country. My parents worked hard to better our lives and they were proud of us and everything they were able to accomplish. So many of my memories are connected to that broken down and yet much-loved house.

As was common at the time, our phone number, Fairlea 459, was both alpha and numeric. It was a land line known locally as a party line because you shared the phone connection with another anonymous household. The two parties could not use the phone line at the same time but if you picked up the phone cautiously and unscrewed the mouthpiece you could listen in on the other person's conversation. Sometimes we would make an odd noise to startle the person. Privacy laws did not exist at the time and it became a source of entertainment for many kids. If you got caught, you hoped the other person never figured out who they were connected to. Unlike today, phones were not a source of entertainment during my childhood. They were a tool that performed a necessary function. No one could have imagined owning a personal phone. That was something you would see in a futuristic movie or in a cartoon. In our limited imaginations it would have taken miles of wire to accomplish that. To connect a phone without a wire seemed implausible.

On wash day, my mother would use the old barrel shaped wringer washing machine. When I was a young child, my misguided sense of curiosity and adventure got my arm caught in the rollers. I wanted to see if I could resist the forces of physics by putting my arm in the moving wringer. Too late, I learned that it was not possible and that the machine would win. The wringer pulled my arm through right up to my shoulder. Luckily, the release popped to set me free, but not before I let out a panicked scream. As I pulled my arm out, I was sure it was going to be flattened. When I realized my arm was intact, my biggest worry was how my mother would discipline me.

Once the clothes came out of the washing machine, Mom would hang the laundry outside on a clothesline that ran from the house to a telephone pole with pulleys at each end. There was a familiar squeak each time mom pulled on the line to pin the next piece of laundry. I would help her hang bedsheets not so much to be useful, but so I could later play hide and seek in them with my friends. After they dried, I would help her fold the sheets as any dutiful son would do.

Just up the road was an industrial laundry business housed in a concrete block building with several tall smoke-stacks. It operated on furnace oil which was common at the time. Through open doors, you could see ladies in white outfits and hair bonnets loading machines with linen and factory uniforms. My mother quickly learned not to hang our clothes out to dry the same day the laundry business was operating. If the wind was in our direction, the soot that spewed out of the smokestacks would settle on the clothes. A rewash would be required. When to do laundry became a game of strategy for our mothers. They had to anticipate what day the laundry business might operate based on the last day that they ran. The time of day was also a crucial part of the calculations. If my mother started her laundry later in the day to make sure the business was not operating, there would not be enough hours of sunlight to dry the clothes. Luckily that business eventually shut down and the property was turned into a treasure trove of discarded mechanical parts for the young adventurers in the neighborhood.

My mother expected her children to help with required household tasks. At our house, whether you were a boy or girl did not factor into how the chores were delegated. From a young age, she taught me domestic skills such as cooking, ironing, washing dishes, vacuuming, and organizing drawers of clothes. At the time it was annoying. I thought girls were supposed to help their mother. That was the deal at my friends' houses. Today I realize that I was fortunate to have a mother that ignored gender lines and accepted norms when teaching and delegating household chores. They are skills and standards that have helped me through the years and that I still use today.

Our house was heated by furnace oil which was contained in a metal tub-like oil tank. It sat next to the back porch and was relatively out of view. We loved watching when the fuel truck would arrive to top up the tank. My younger brother Joe and cousin Claudio thought the tank was filled with water. One hot summer day they decided to quench their thirst by opening the drain valve and drinking the furnace oil thinking it was water. This lack of judgement sent both of them to the hospital to get their stomachs pumped. After this they learned to use the garden hose if they were thirsty.

There were plenty of neighbors from various countries on Martin Drive. German families lived on either side of us. One family made soap from animal lard and grew rhubarb in a far corner of the yard. We would raid the garden when we thought they were not looking. An entire season was dedicated to picking rhubarb, running away, and finding a secret spot to eat our contraband without detection. It was not until early the next season that I learned the hard way that rhubarb is too sour to eat before it ripens. But it was not only their garden that was of interest to us. Their son Roland was popular because of his full collection of Beatle albums. His brother Willy was my partner in crime. Dutch and Scottish families rounded out the ethnic diversity. My father would say that we had the United Nations living on our street. It was normal to be an immigrant on Martin Drive.

My father had his own large vegetable garden in our postage stamp size yard. Dressed in his customary white tank top, he spent countless hours cultivating tomatoes, lettuce, zucchini, and carrots. He also loved to grow flowers, especially roses. The pops of color from the scattered flower beds broke up the monotony of the green grass. He was proud of his gardens and spent much of his free time tending to them whether they needed attention or not. This was his nirvana. In hindsight, I think this was his escape from the day-to-day craziness that came with four spirited kids in the house.

In a far corner of the garden, we had a steel forty-five-gallon burn barrel where all the flammables and garbage were set on fire. Watching the refuse burn was exciting. We would sit around the fire and watch in awe as the flames reached astronomical heights. When cinders would pop and fly into the air, it was like having fireworks in our backyard. With our imaginations we could turn even the disposal of refuse into an exciting event.

A tall and stately willow tree that my father had planted a few years earlier now blanketed the middle of the yard. It hung low and wide and provided much needed shade during hot summer afternoons. That is where we played Tarzan, swinging from branch to branch. The yard was eventually encircled with hedges. Once a week, we mustered up all the strength that we had and took turns pushing a heavy old rotary grass cutter across the lawn. We helped one another budge the contraption free when it got stuck. When my father could finally afford a used gas-powered lawnmower, that arduous task became much easier, but sadly, the teamwork ended.

Our loose gravel and sand driveway butted up against our neighbor's property. After each oil change my dad would spread the old engine oil up and down the driveway to keep the dust down. Today, that would not be considered a good practice but back then it was perfectly acceptable. Our family car was proudly parked in the driveway. It was an old black '49 Dodge four door sedan with bubbled-out fenders and an off green roof. We did not own this vehicle because it was the car of my father's dreams. We owned it because a used '49 Chrysler product was inexpensive, and we were able to purchase it at a reasonable price. Bragging rights came from simply owning the vehicle. The firm bench style seats were protected by fitted clear plastic covers that would stick to your body on hot summer days. The radio was AM only and the windows had to be manually cranked open. The headlight dimmer button was located on the floor near your left foot and as you may have guessed, it was foot operated.

The old '49 housed a flat head six banger with so much room under the hood you could hide a family in it. It was just a basic engine with a few wires. On the column was the three-speed gear shifter. The steering wheel was huge and resembled a planetary model with two or three orbits and a large sun in the middle where the horn was located. This was the era of understated and simple features in cars. To clean the inside of the vehicle you simply opened the door and sprayed water from your garden hose on the floor mats.

The doors were then left open for drying. It sounds crazy in today's world, but it worked back then. Many years later the '49 Dodge was traded up to a white tail winged '59 Plymouth with a push button shift. I always wished we had a truck but back in those days they were meant for the farm and to be used only as utility vehicles.

Despite all the function and affordability of the '49 Chrysler family car, my father did have a dream vehicle. Having grown up in Italy, he was a big fan of the FIAT. It was something that he would see from time to time on the streets of his village but not something that he ever thought would be attainable by a poor farm boy. FIAT was and still is the largest car manufacturer in Italy. The name FIAT is an acronym for "Fabbrica Italiana Automobili Torino". Production began in Turin in 1899 and in 1910 a new facility was built in Poughkeepsie New York.

My father's dream came true when he managed to procure a 1950 FIAT 600 from an Italian friend who was fed up with it. He loved this car. Outside of his family, there was nothing that gave him more joy. It was proudly and safely parked at the top of the driveway in front of the family car. It had a 600 cubic centimeter engine that sat in the back. The engine placement and its appearance were similar to a Volkswagen bug. It had a powder blue exterior with a beige interior. On weekends and in the evenings, he liked to tinker with his pride and joy. He finally got it running but it was always breaking down and in need of scarce and expensive parts. That eventually ended the love affair my father had with the car. It was not long before it was towed away but not before I managed to get a few rides in it.

I loved going places with my father. He would always ask if I wanted to accompany him. Of course I did. As a young boy, it was an honor to go anywhere with him. He was my role model and hero. Often our drives would be visits with his brothers or a friend. I remember the rides through town and for some strange reason I remember how I enjoyed the smell of bus fumes. Maybe it was because we did not have many buses in town and the fumes were a strange and unique smell. Maybe the fumes made me feel like I was going somewhere far away from Martin Drive.

Occasionally on weekends, Dad would treat us to a movie but with a bit of a twist. He would begin by taking us for a ride along the county roads and we would eventually wind up near the drive-in theater. Seatbelts were not mandatory, and we would lie on the back dash under the rear window as Dad drove around. After picking a good vantage point, he would pull to the side of the dirt road and manually crank down the windows. From there, we could hear the distant sound of the movie and watch the show through the open windows. The screen was so far away that it would be like viewing a movie on an iPhone these days. We loved those nights and we felt privileged to share those moments with our Mom and Dad.

We were of modest means but there was always plenty of good food on Martin Drive. Milk, eggs, and bread would be delivered to the house and Mom canned pears, tomatoes, peaches, and an Italian stew called 'melanzana' which was made of eggplant and a blend of various vegetables. Harvest time was spent helping Mom fill glass mason jars and boiling them in tubs of water to seal the lids. Dad oversaw making wine and sausage while mom would make pasta, polenta, lasagna and my favorite, gnocchi. Weekends filled with cooking and preserving never seemed like a chore. Rather it seemed like pleasant recreational time spent with my parents.

All the cooking, canning, and preserving was done mostly out of financial necessity but also due to a preference for freshly made food. Life in our Italian home was centered on homemade, wholesome, natural food, coupled with cellar stored wine. Back then, most Italians did not want to buy more expensive processed food and prepared dinners from the grocery store. Even If they could afford it, they would have thought it was a waste of money for substandard food. Dad would take a slice of processed white bread, roll it into a large marble sized ball of dough and would then say, "That's not bread." The only way we could have a well-stocked kitchen at minimal cost was to put the effort into the preparation.

As a young child, I would help my mother make the gnocchi. This is also when my mother would try to improve my Italian language skills. Mom would teach me to count in Italian as we itemized all the ingredients. She would bring out the big plywood board that all the pasta was made on. Dad had bought a sheet of three-eighth inch plywood for that purpose. When it was time to make pasta, the board would be placed on the kitchen table and it covered the entire surface. Pasta making would fill an otherwise potentially boring morning with activity. To prepare, the first thing we did was boil the potatoes in a large pot. After they were well cooked and taking care not to burn ourselves, we would peel the skins off and mash them to a pulp. Next, the flour, water and eggs were mixed in with the potato mash. My mother would tell me that the egg and the love that we put into it glued everything together.

I would help Mom knead and roll the huge potato and flour boulder on the plywood board. We would then create a depression in the doughy ball where she filled it with her secret ingredients. She would say she was adding the eye of a newt and the toe of a frog. I knew this was not true, but it was fun to pretend that it was. We would then mix it all together and reshape the ball of dough. After sprinkling flour on it, we would flatten it out with the old wooden rolling pin. Next, we would carefully cut long slender strips. These strips would be rolled then clipped about every inch making a small tidbit. We did this repeatedly until all the strips of dough were reduced to tiny pieces. Finally, came the fun part where we would push our fingers into that little piece of dough to make the dumpling. The gnocchi were ready to drop into a pot of boiling water.

Once the dumplings were cooked and drained, my mother would submerge them into her homemade sauce or 'sugo'. The sugo would take all day to make. Simmering throughout the day, the aroma of the tomatoes, meat and spices would permeate the house. The sugo always started with sliced cloves of garlic sizzling in a pot with a drizzle of olive oil over a low flame. The aroma of the garlic as it cooked and turned brown was unmistakable and so fragrant that you could barely wait for dinner to happen. This sauce was also used on her thick doughy pizzas. It was exciting to be able to add the toppings. To this day, anytime I enter a restaurant and smell garlic simmering it takes me back to my mother's kitchen and the times that she allowed me to be her sous chef.

Another of her delicacies was her homegrown, home-made roasted peppers. After picking them from the garden, Mom would place them on the gas stove grill top before lighting an element. We did not have electric igniters back then. A match or rolled up paper towel with a small flame would be probed into the gas element resulting in a burst of blue flame. She would rotate the peppers over the flame until they had black peeling skin. She always allowed me to remove the outer flaky skin before tearing the peppers into strips. She would then add her secret spices and oil to get them ready for canning. My mother has never revealed what these secret spices are, but Colonel Sanders' recipe does not compare with my mother's exquisitely spiced mouthwatering peppers.

Another of my mother's creations required five pounds of flour, two cups of water, a packet of yeast, and a tablespoon of anisette. My mother magically turned this into a crusty bagel-like dough, and then baked it in a twisted rope circle shape. We called it 'ciamelli'. I loved the taste of this original Italian bread because of the firm texture and the hint of anisette flavor.

The only thing I liked more than cooking was eating my mother's culinary delights. I was a young boy with a huge appetite. After I finished my plate, I would scavenge for anything that was left over. Gnocchi, insalata or ciamelli were my favorite meals. Salad was crisp iceberg lettuce, onions, carrots, and peppers soaked with oil and vinegar and a sprinkle of salt. With the crusty bread, I would soak up the last bit of sauce and the remaining salad. My mother believed in the power of olive oil and the power of food. She believed good cooking brought not only good health but also happiness. The kitchen was always the hub of our home.

The rule of the house was that everyone had to be present for dinner. As we got older, we were allowed to skip other meals during the day or eat in front of the television, but dinner was as sacred as religion. It was usually a time of reflection, sharing and bonding as a family. We did not leave the table until everyone was done eating and most of the food was consumed. This rule was probably a result of my parents' wartime experiences when food was often scarce.

Leftovers were rare in our house and dinner was usually our only opportunity to enjoy that day's culinary extravaganza. For this reason alone, we did not want to miss dinner.

We loved to share our homemade delicacies with family and friends and we regularly had relatives over to enjoy a table laden with all the gastronomical treats. With the feast, there would also be plenty of loud and boisterous talk. When adult guests came over, Mom would bring out an assortment of cheeses, olives, and baked goods. Dad would fill glasses with his homemade wine insisting that guests stay a little longer and 'manga'. He would then entice you with Grappa, Limoncello or Millefiori. This would routinely continue into the evening. Wineglasses were small tumblers rather than stemmed glassware. They would invite friends over for a 'bicchiereen' (small tumbler) of wine rather than a glass of wine. The drinks would loosen up the vocal cords and stories of the old country would be bandied about. When the homemade wine ran out, my father would bring out half gallon bottles of the low cost, Italian favorite Carlo Rossi wine. After those half gallon jugs were empty, my father would go down to the basement and refill the bottles with the homemade wine that was fermenting in oak barrels. In the meantime, the young kids would be running through the house crazed with excitement, hyped up on sugar.

As I grew older, I realized that my friends loved to come over not so much to see me but because they knew Mom would put her apron on and prepare a feast for them. My mother loved to fuss over my friends. No one left our house hungry. Some of my friends would show up even if I was not home knowing Mom would not let them leave until they had broken bread and filled their bellies with capicola, cheese, salami, and wine. I believe that some of my friendships were cemented by my mother's food.

The only time we had ice cream in the house was when we had guests over, and I LOVED ice cream. On one of those occasions my mother's older sister, my Aunt Amelia, was visiting with her husband and kids. My aunt picked me up and sat me on the kitchen counter where she fed me a huge soup spoon of vanilla ice cream. In my excitement, I swallowed the whole scoop at once. That delicious vanilla treat shot straight to my head. The next thing I remember is waking up on the couch. My mother and my aunt were anxiously chattering in Italian. The anxiety quickly turned to relief. We did not know that eating too much ice cream at once not only gives you brain freeze, but it can stop your brain all together. It was a lesson learned.

These family gatherings would rotate amongst the aunts and uncles. Since my father had six of his siblings here and my mother had one, there were plenty of these family gatherings each weekend. Mom and Dad also had several cousins who had crossed the Atlantic and lived nearby. As our circle of cousins expanded, so did our circle of best friends. We were never without someone to play with or keep ourselves entertained with.

An Italian wedding was always like a family reunion on steroids. Every wedding, regardless of who was getting married was a big deal. Preparation for the day was an all-encompassing weeklong process. After the invitation was received, the next step was to plan for the wedding day. Nice clothes and impeccably dressed children were important to make a good impression. A suit, a tie and fancy shoes were mandatory attire for the boys while fancy dresses for the girls was expected party wear. Gold jewelry was worn by all. This gold was not your standard ten or fourteen carat gold. We had eighteen carat gold jewelry from Italy. The number of carats in the gold was a status symbol and a source of pride.

On the day of the wedding, excitement would fill the air as we all dressed in our best attire for the culinary and entertainment extravaganza that lay ahead. Most times, I did not even know who the wedding couples were. All I knew was that they were in some way related to my mother or father. Wedding gifts were not wrapped packages. What guests brought to the wedding was a 'la Busta' or envelope with a congratulations card and a stack of cash to help the couple start a life together. Italian weddings were large and usually held at The Roma Club in one of their spacious and elaborately decorated ballrooms.

Wine, food, and song played a key role in Italian weddings and they all flowed freely. My father enjoyed his wine, although I never saw him get drunk. He usually worked himself into a joyful buzz which seemed to bring out his playful side. He was a changed person once he had a couple glasses of wine. I suspect the wine eased the burden of his day-to-day responsibilities and it gave him permission to let loose and enjoy himself. He would entertain the family and guests with absurd and ridiculous stories.

After several rounds at the open bar, an announcement would be made to take your seat for dinner. The feast typically began with 'Stracciatella', a soup of egg drops and broth. Next came the spaghetti and meatballs followed by generous helpings of roasted chicken and potatoes, breaded pieces of beef on a stick known as city chicken, cutlets, steamed vegetables, and bread. Random speeches would interrupt the sumptuous, seemingly never-ending meal. The main course would be followed by a garden salad. In our culture, the salad was always served last. Italian belief is to enjoy the good food first and not spoil your appetite with a

starter like salad. Dessert was typically a cannoli followed
with coffee or tea. It was a meal fit for a medieval King or
an average Italian family.

Later, when the food was cleared away the tables were
pushed to the edges of the room and the music began. The
adult guests mingled, drank, and danced. The kids slid
around on the dance floor in their stocking feet. Everyone
caught up on the latest news and the day was always a joyful
occasion. When the evening faded it was time to grab your
'bomboniere'. This was the typical wedding favor made up
of half a dozen white hard shelled sugar-coated almonds in
a traditional small porcelain container. Along with your
'bomboniere' there was a paper plate filled with desserts and
a couple pieces of city chicken. The plate was covered with
a napkin rather than tin foil for protection. With these treats
in hand, it was time to head home. Leaving in the wee hours
of the morning, we were exhausted but too excited to sleep.
We could not wait for the next wedding.

My father was not known to swear often. When angered,
his favorite blasphemy was 'God Damnit' or 'Jesus Christ'.
Either of these phrases were enough to make me cringe and
wait for that bolt of lightning to strike. I knew it was not
cool to take the Lord's name in vain, but it was his go to
swear. Driving into town one Saturday evening, a cat ran in
front of the car. Dad tried valiantly to avoid hitting it but
was unsuccessful. We both grimaced as we felt the tires pass
over the poor creature. Next, out of my father's mouth came
a word that was never spoken in our house. It was that most
vile of words that I never expected to hear my deeply
respected father utter - "F**k."

Immediately he became angry with himself for uttering
the infamous, forbidden 'F word'. Without pause, I heard
him say, "God Damnit, Jesus Christ! I just had confession

yesterday!" I was shocked and sat silent, afraid to move and cause more swearwords to spew from his mouth. That was the one and only time I ever heard my dad use such a colorful string of expletives. That was when I realized that my father was a regular human being rather than a deity.

As a young boy eager to emulate his father, I would attempt to imitate his eating habits. Mom would make a cabbage stew-like soup and Dad and I would bite into a large, peeled onion followed by a scoop of the soup. It took some getting used to, but it eventually became common practice for me. When my mother made pasta, he and I would cover the pasta with a heavy sprinkling of hot chili peppers. It would burn going down, but I loved sharing this practice with my dad. He would always challenge me to try eating strange things in peculiar ways. He turned my love of food into an adventure.

However, there were some food choices that I found unacceptable and downright unpalatable. One was his morning ritual. I would gag when he poked a hole in each end of a raw egg and then sucked it clean out of one end. It was disgusting. Dad said that was how his father taught him to eat eggs while growing up on the farm. This practice would stop with my father. There was nothing in the world that he could bribe me with to even try it.

There was also another tradition I struggled with. A couple of times a year I accompanied my father and two other neighborhood Italians to a pig farm on a remote country road. There my dad and his friends met with the owner who would direct us to a pen. We pushed our way through snorting pigs that were outraged with our presence. The smell was so disgusting that I had to pinch my nose and pull my shirt up over my nostrils to dull the odor of pig dung.

One of the men shouted "Questo!" which translated to English as "This one."

We all gathered near the pig he chose, and the men seemed to agree that it was indeed the one. There was some chatter that took place in Italian that I did not fully understand. The prize pig was then shuffled out of the pen into a containment area. There the farmer pulled out a long, shiny knife and quickly stabbed the pig in the throat. As it fell to the ground blood squirted out of the wound. Immediately they tied the pig's back legs together, hung it upside down and raised it up with a hook that was attached to the rafters. The poor dead animal's blood poured into a large metal container. After about fifteen minutes the carcass was lowered and taken outside where it was placed on a pile of wood. Next, the wood pile was set ablaze with the pig lying in the middle. As a young child, it was horrifying to watch. I was told the fire was needed to burn off all the hair on the pig's skin. After the fire cooled, the burnt dead pig was loaded onto the truck bed.

We drove to a house where the pig was carried into a shed and placed on a large table. The carcass was again hoisted up by its back legs and the men went about the butchering process. This was going to feed three families with bacon, capicola and sausage or 'salsiccia' as it was well known to Italians. With a wide mischievous grin, one of the men offered the full pig bladder to one of the curious kids watching the process. That lucky child chased the rest of us with the full bladder, squirting us with pig urine as we ran away screaming in terror.

Sausage making came after the carcass was fully butchered. The raw meat and bits of fat would be ground in a hand cranked meat grinder while spices such as pepper flakes were added. It was then pushed into the intestine skins. As the meat exited the grinder it would be twisted every three inches into a neat string of sausage. The sausage links would be hung to dry, age and cure. Over time the red sausage would cure to a lighter brown color. It was then that we knew it was ready to eat. Unlike many of my friends at school, I knew that food did not just appear in a grocery store. I had hands on knowledge about homemade food and making meals from scratch. But that was not all. I also knew about a vile Italian secret that was unknown to my American born counterparts.

On Sunday mornings, my father would wake us from our sweet dreams, order us to get dressed in our Sunday best and go to church with him. Mom would stay home and work diligently to have dinner ready when we returned. At church, I would tap my fingers on the pew to whatever beat I could hear in my head. The Priest was preaching in Latin. Dad would invariably smack my fingers to stop the tapping. I had absolutely no idea what was being said and it was difficult to sit through an hour of utter boredom. After all, how could I benefit from the Priest's words when I could not understand what he was saying. I would follow my dad's lead as he stood, kneeled, or sat down. Pangs of hunger would overtake my body long before church ended. Dreaming about what my mother was cooking would get me through the ordeal.

Sunday dinner was usually homemade pasta and meatballs, which I loved. However, not every Sunday dinner was as enticing and appetizing. There was a disgusting aberration that would occur every year around Easter. When we returned home from church, we did not breathe in the comforting smells of my mother's pasta and homemade bread. Instead, a putrid, acrid odor permeated the air. It was so disgusting that words do not exist in the English or

Italian languages to describe how offensive the odor was. As a child, it was horrifying to think that my loving mother would want her child to eat something so vile. It was a smell that would send me into convulsions and force me to take a stand against my wonderful mother's cooking.

I have two vivid childhood memories of Palm Sunday. The first memory is a pleasant one. At church we would receive a palm branch to take home. In the car we would bat each other with the fronds until my father would yell at us to cut it out. It was meant to be placed over a wall hanging of the Virgin Mary's likeness. In our case, it was hung over the plaque that I had naively used as a dartboard. That is my happy recollection.

My second memory takes me back to the noxious smell of my mother's cooking on that particular day. It was at those times of the year that the air in the house was filled with the dreaded odor of 'Baccala' when we got home from church. I had to tell her that the smell of her cooking made me want to throw up. Salted cod cooking on the stove emitted an aroma that was unmistakable and one that I came to despise. On those days there were many strained discussions with my parents about what I would or would not eat. I saw it as taking a stand on what I was physically able to ingest and not regurgitate. For me, it was more of an issue of what I could eat as opposed to what I would eat. Unfortunately, my parents did not see it that way. They saw it as rebellion via food. Being the ever-obedient son, I would make the attempt, but I did have to draw my line in the sand. I would force anything that even came remotely in contact with the fish down my throat with a grimace, squinted eyes, and a beverage. My parents saw it as immature theatrics. I saw it as avoiding death.

As a youngster, when I got myself into a troubling situation, I would hear that familiar phrase from Mom, "Aspetta che tuo padre torni a casa" meaning, wait until your father gets home. Dad worked at the factory sterilizing tin cans of processed foods in large steel pressure vessels which he called 'retorts.' Steam would be pumped in to kill the bad bacteria after he loaded case after case of unboxed cans into the gigantic vats. It was a stressful job since he always had to be conscious of potential disaster if he drove the forklift carelessly or failed to set the steam settings correctly. Being a senior employee, he usually worked the day shift and would arrive home just before dinner in his uniform, smelling like cooked tomatoes holding his black flip top metal lunch pail. This is when my mother would give him her daily briefing about what went right or wrong that day. His schedule was perfect for punishment if the day warranted it. What a way to spoil a kid's day. How could you think of anything else knowing that your future on this planet would be in question once he got home?

Depending on the severity of my misbehavior, my father would either give me a stern look or a look verging on seething anger. If it was the angry look, I knew he would be going for the belt around his waist. He was surprisingly good at taking it off in one pull. This is when I would try to take refuge between Mom and the counter as she washed dishes or prepared dinner. When he came after me, there was this game of shifting from one side of Mom to the other as he tried to grab me. I could usually out fox him at this point. I would run up the stairs and into my bedroom closet that was protected only by a hanging curtain. My parents' bedroom was on the main floor next to the kitchen. I had convinced myself that my father could not climb those stairs because he was too old and tired to make the trek up to the second floor. In my young mind this was why my parents' bedroom was on the first floor separate from us kids. It made perfect sense. If he did manage the climb, I had an escape route that would involve crawling out the bedroom window, onto the porch roof, down the column and off to freedom.

It was years later that I finally figured out that my thirty something year old father was a good actor, and he knew how to use fear effectively. Mom and Dad must have had a good laugh after those episodes. He never did touch me, my two sisters or brother but he sure scared us. I can still see that look as he pulled off his belt and hear the terrifying swishing sound that it made. Thankfully, there were not too many of those belt pulling episodes. Since I was a boy and the oldest in our family and the extended family, Mom would always remind me that I was in an influential and honorary position. It was my duty to be respectful, set a good example and stay out of trouble. I knew I could not bring disgrace to my family.

Years later, when I was much older, my mother would say, "Vai a trovare le tuo zia e tuo zio" which meant go visit your aunts and uncles. She would always remind me that I was the oldest of the cousins and I had to go as a show of respect. This put a lot of pressure on me. How was I to become a carefree kid when I was being groomed with all this first-born protocol? This was the cross that I had to bear. I had to tow the family line, but I also wanted to be a popular kid which sometimes meant stepping over that fine line.

Dad was by nature a fun-loving guy who enjoyed spending time with his kids. He would take us to the beach where we would get into splashing fights and chase each other through the waves. He would pull us through the water on those oversized black inner tubes that were so common before the modern day floaty. He would refer to bikini clad girls as "barenaket" ladies with a slight Italian accent. Who knew that one day a popular band would actually use that name? I still chuckle when I hear that phrase because it brings back happy memories.

In June of each year, the company that my father worked for would sponsor a family picnic filled with games, rides, and food. Dad and I would stroll around the fair-like atmosphere and test our skills at the fishpond attraction and ride the Ferris Wheel. Times were simpler and children could roam freely and aimlessly. Stranger danger was not seen as the ever-present threat that it is today. We were told not to take candy from a stranger, but beyond that we were happily oblivious to any sort of danger. Looking back, I realize the threat was probably there, but we were not as keenly aware of it as we are now. Today, extensive television broadcasting and readily available information on the internet has made us more aware of potential peril. It also sometimes contributes to imagined paranoia that does not exist. In retrospect, I realize that I grew up in a time of ignorant bliss.

When I was still in elementary school my father would send me without adult supervision on a twenty-minute walk into town to buy him a pack of cigarettes. The destination was always T-K's Discount, where his favorite brand 'Export A' was the least expensive. At that time, age restrictions were not in effect, so it seemed like a perfectly normal thing to do. As I got older and smoking laws were enacted those trips to the store ended.

I was also my mother's mule. She would give me a box top, some money and send me to Ward's corner store. I was told to hand the piece of cardboard to the storekeeper, and he would give me what I needed to take home. She never told me what it was that I was buying. In my young mind, I was convinced that I was on some top-secret mission buying forbidden contraband. My mother has since confessed that she was sending me to buy feminine pads. Luckily, I was oblivious to what my cargo was. And thankfully, I did not cross paths with any friends that did.

As my youngest sister Paula grew older, she would be enlisted in a weekly ritual that I was exempted from. My mother would yell "Beauty Shop – Beauty Shop" whenever she needed her hair combed or pinned. Paula was always ready and willing to play the role of beautician and hair stylist. I think that was one of the foundations that their beautiful lifelong relationship was built on. To this day, Mom still relies on Paula for guidance and support.

Only once did my mother drag me to her hairdresser. I waited patiently while they dyed and dried her hair under those giant head cones. The hairdresser asked me to go to the back room where he wanted to show me magazines. It felt weird and I promptly turned away and moved so I could be within my mother's scope of vision. At the time I was too afraid to tell my parents about the incident for fear that they would not believe me. Many years later, that hairdresser was charged as a sex offender after one of his assistants filed a complaint. My parents were shocked. That incident taught me as a parent to make sure that my children knew they had a voice should they encounter any unusual predicament. I made sure they knew that even though I was a parent, they could approach me and trust me to share even the worst of news.

As kids, we found adventure in the local forests and creeks, leaving home early in the morning, and not returning until daylight dimmed, or a parent called out from the front porch. The loudest parent was usually the Italian lady up the street who would give a loud shout out for her son Anatoli, or Andy as we knew him. For some reason, her voice could pierce the air like no other mother's voice could. The neighborhood kids would stop what they were doing when they heard her bellow. All activity would cease, and we would literally freeze in that moment. Even if our mothers had already called us once or even twice, we knew that when Andy's mom yelled it was probably a good time for all of us to head home.

The world outside our door was where we found our entertainment. We were free to develop our imagination and create a world of adventure and make believe. Martin Drive was the perfect environment for young kids filled with energy and curiosity. We lived in actual reality, not virtual reality. Hours would be spent lying on the lawn looking up at the treetops as the leaves fluttered in the wind. We enjoyed watching the cloud formations. In these fluffy shapes we saw imaginary animals as they billowed and merged into one another. We spent many innocent hours climbing trees and riding our bikes through the neighborhoods. On hot days Dad would set up the twirling sprinkler so we could cool off and chase each other through the spray. When we heard the musical jingle of the Dickie Dee ice cream truck, we would rush to be first in line leaving a trail of water and wet footprints on the sidewalk.

My magnifying glass would entertain me for hours. For some yet to be understood reason, burning holes through wood and paper fascinated me. As a budding entomologist, I would drown ants in a glass of water and then pour them out onto the sidewalk. With brilliant sunshine and a magnifying glass, I could generate a ray of hot light, aim it at the drowned ants and watch them come back to life again. However, one day karma came to even the score.

One hot afternoon as the sprinklers were being primed,

I raced home through the front door and up the stairs to slip into my bathing suit. Changing quickly, I ran out the door already imagining the spray of the cool water. All of a sudden, I felt a horrible stinging pain coming from inside my swimsuit. I opened the front of my bathing suit and out flew a bee. I peered down at my manhood and watched as a small sack of venom was swelling around a stinger nicely lodged where no bee should ever have landed. How in the heck did that bee get into my pants? I reached down, carefully prodded the stinger out and then ran to the bathroom in search of alcohol or iodine to kill the pain. The trauma of that attack stayed with me for a long time. It was years before I put a bathing suit on without doing a full inspection first. I was sure that this was Mother Nature getting back at me.

The advent of the Beatles inspired us to make guitars out of balsa wood and form bands fashioned after our favorite singing group. We thought we looked and sounded just like John, Paul, Ringo, and George even though we obviously did not. Our instruments were not capable of producing sound so we would simulate guitar acoustics with our voices. We held concerts for the local kids, charging a nickel for admittance to what we promoted as a concert. We were holding a balsa wood concert on November 22, 1963 when the devastating news broke about President John F. Kennedy. We were young but we knew something bad had happened based on our parents' reactions. In the evening, we got wrapped up in the television coverage with the adults. This would be the day that we put our guitars down and the day that our pretend music careers ended.

Windy days provided another opportunity for entertainment. We made kites using paper or plastic bags and one-quarter inch wide sticks that we bought at the hardware store. With a ball of string, some paint, and a good breeze we would fill the sky with our colorful kites as we chased one another through the fields. If the kite was not perfectly balanced, it would suffer a Kamikaze nosedive, falling straight down from a precarious launch, piercing the ground, and shattering the entire framework. It took many attempts before we would perfect a kite that could actually fly. I think we found the challenge of the build just as exciting as the kite taking flight. Our imaginations soared with every kite that we built and were able to keep in the sky. We were always dreaming of the next more improved model that we could make.

It was unheard of for Italian kids to get an allowance, so it was imperative that we find some way to make pocket change. Unlike current times, opportunities for young kids to earn money were limited. Jobs at restaurants and grocery stores were filled by adults. Fast food establishments were non-existent in our little town. The only real opportunity was in agriculture or farm work. It was common for children of incredibly young ages to be seen at local farms picking beans or tomatoes. It was also common practice to place stones or dirt on the bottom of the basket so it would fill up faster. This was important because if we managed to fill an entire container, we would earn twenty-five cents. This was enough money to go to Vick's corner store and buy some sweet treats. We could purchase several grab bags of candy for two cents each. Grab bags were a tiny bag filled with mixed varieties of candies such as mojos, gum, and jawbreakers. As I made one particularly large purchase, I remember old Vick telling me that I owed him ten cents, not a dime. He told me a dime was too much like saying 'damn'. Back then adults were not afraid to straighten out kids and they did it freely.

Occasionally as young aspiring entrepreneurs seeking other forms of income, we would covertly raid the local corn field and fill a bushel with sweet corn. We would then head over to a busy street corner and set up business. As brazen as this sounds, strangely enough no one ever questioned where we got the corn. They were just excited to buy mouth-watering locally grown sweet corn at rock bottom prices.

We amused ourselves with endless streams of jokes and frightened ourselves with ghost stories that we conjured up. Many of our imaginary ghosts were disfigured and were missing limbs. Most of our humor included ethnic or racial connotations. Our stories and jokes would not be funny in today's world of inclusivity and acceptance. Despite being taught otherwise at home and at school, these slurs seemed acceptable.

Even with all the freedom that we had, there were lines that could not be crossed. I learned this very quickly at a young age when I got in trouble with the law. My friends and I were fascinated with guns. However, except for hunting, they did not exist in our world. We figured out how to create a makeshift gun out of a short piece of copper or steel pipe and a carved wooden handle. The pipe diameter had to be just wide enough to slip in a lit firecracker, aim and fire. You had to time it exactly right or risk blowing your fingertips off. My fatal error was pointing it at another kid.

After he received a face full of red firecracker paper and gunpowder, he ran off screaming in terror. I ran home acting like nothing happened. With the inevitable knock on the door, my worst fear was realized. There stood the local policeman. In my young mind I thought he was going to handcuff me and drag me off to prison. Fearfully hiding behind my mother, I listened intently to his warning. I was relieved to learn there would be no jail time. It was a close call, and I swore I would never do it again. This should have been the end of the story except I still had to deal with my mother. She was not impressed with my delinquent behavior. Rather than being angry, she was visibly sad. How could she raise a son like this? What had she done wrong? She did not punish me or tell my father, but her disappointment was more of a deterrent for future bad behavior than the police. It was a close call, and that day marked the end of my fascination with guns.

However, it did not mark the end of my interest in explosives and fire. There was a period when I was a bit of a pyromaniac. For some crazy reason, setting things on fire was exciting to me and my friends. I remember inadvertently setting off a brushfire when I placed a firecracker into the crack of a wooden telephone pole. Had I known that creosote was flammable I may have taken a different approach. Even though I was gripped with fear, it was exciting to watch the firetrucks arrive with sirens wailing and lights blazing. They quickly put the fire out and then asked who started it. We all stood there shrugging our shoulders. In our circle this was known as the Italian salute. I had dodged another close call.

One other time I decided the tiny homemade shed I made should be soaked with gas and lit on fire. I have no rational explanation as to why I thought this would be a good idea. The shed was built out of random scraps of wood to protect my pushcart from the elements. Evidently, I did not realize that I needed to protect it from myself. As the flames grew and spread towards the evergreen tree, I got a bit worried. It was time to turn the garden hose on and save the day. I will never understand why I was so fascinated with fire. Thankfully, my pyromania phase passed before I did any real damage, and our house was spared a toasty roasting. We were a mischievous and curious bunch of kids, but mostly we were just bored and a bit naive about cause and effect.

Being a kid with an abundance of energy meant always looking for new things to do to fill the long days and evenings. My neighbor Willy and I devised a plan where we would outfit ourselves in capes and masks like superheroes and prowl the night looking through neighbors' windows. Many hours and much energy went into creating the costume and devising our plan. It went relatively well until one fateful night when I was boosted up in my sidekick's cupped hands and peered into a window as we had already done many times before. I reported to Willy that a man was sitting in a chair watching television. I then reported to him that the man got up and left the room. It was only then that I realized we had to make a quick exit. Unfortunately, it was too late.

Suddenly, he appeared around the corner of the house and we scrambled in opposite directions, both of us running for our lives. We disappeared into the cornfield. Breathless and scared, I continued running for what felt like hours. I waited until I was confident that the immediate danger had passed. Eventually I circled back to my house where I met up with Willy once again. Still in our capes, his white and mine black, we exchanged horror stories about the event. At that point I was focused on not knowing whether my parents would find out what happened and what my fate would eventually be. He was focused on the ass kicking he received from the man. Now that our plot had been uncovered and exposed, we decided that it was time to retire as superhero villains. For whatever reason, my parents never found out what happened that night.

A massive, two story barn, clad with dark grey weathered wood sat across the field from our house. The rustic structure sat in a small pasture amongst several tall trees. It was always locked up and for the kids in the neighborhood, it conjured up visions of scary adventures and hidden treasures. One fateful day, we noticed that the door was open and a few of us ventured inside. We found ourselves in a dark spider webbed alternate universe. Inside, the structure was made of heavy hand-hewn lumber. Some still retained its original round tree trunk cylindrical form. The sun peaked through the wood and gave us enough light to see what treasures were strewn about. As we slowly made our way through the first floor, we found a seemingly endless number of relics. There were piles of dusty torn books that we imagined were chewed up by mice. Old rusty farm implements, and dilapidated furniture filled the massive space. On the second floor, we found a scale model of a house built on a four by eight-foot sheet of plywood. It was a detailed and meticulous model using wood, putty, and stones. Even the windows and doors were hand made. Deciding to end our adventure for fear of getting caught, we left and agreed to come back sometime in the future providing it was once again left unlocked.

The next day I ventured back into the still unlocked barn on my own. This time it looked like the barn had been vandalized. Everything had been thrown around and appeared ruined. Books and papers were torn and ripped out of their covers. Even the model house had sustained massive damage. It was sad to see all the destruction. Wishing I had carted off some of the small treasures the day before, I managed to salvage one small book signed and dated in the late 1800s. It was a child's story book. I took it home with me, tucked it under my mattress and kept it as a memento of that sad day.

Despite my fire starter phase, my stint as a Peeping Tom and the breaking and entering, my life and experiences on Martin Drive helped me develop into a law-abiding citizen. My most enduring and treasured memories of my childhood are from this phase in my life and the time that I shared with my parents, aunts, uncles, and friends. The adventures enriched my life. The misadventures had enough of an impact to steer me in the right direction. What I did wrong taught me what to do right. My parents' and extended family's constant presence and involvement provided a positive, secure base to model my life on. I did not realize it at the time, but not all of my friends were that fortunate.

4

SCHOLASTIC ADVENTURES

Entering grade one as a Catholic kid in the Public School system proved to be a difficult but necessary transition. Just by virtue of being Catholic, I was different. I had two strikes prohibiting me from blending in – my ethnicity and my religion. I was never enrolled in kindergarten so this little Italian boy, surrounded mostly by Italian speaking adults, had some catching up to do.

It was here that I eventually learned to recite the ABCs. If you managed to get through A to Z, you would receive that cherished gold star next to your name on a yellow eight and a half by eleven sheets of paper pinned high above the chalk board for the whole class to see. By the end of the year, my classmates had countless stars plastered on their cards concealing the paper they were stuck to. In contrast, my yellow sheet had plenty of open space on it. You could count the stars on two hands. My very patient teacher never gave up on me though, and in June I left grade one having conquered the basics of the alphabet. After the firm foundation and eventual confidence I developed that year, my academic struggles did not seem as monumental anymore. I was no longer a little Italian boy in an English class. Rather, I was just another little boy in class. The assimilation process had begun.

After several more nondescript years of schooling, in grade six, I eagerly volunteered and was chosen to deliver lunch milk to students throughout the school. This coveted chore allowed me to miss some class time. You had to have the teacher's confidence and permission for this privilege. Everyone wanted the honor of delivering milk, but few were chosen. Each class had to place their milk order first thing in the morning, and it was my job, along with a few fellow students, to fill those orders. We felt important as we loaded stout little glass bottles of milk into metal frame cages, placed them on wagons and then delivered them from class to class.

However, after the deliveries were done, lunchtime always devolved into an embarrassing 'show and tell' period for me. My parents did not believe in grocery store white bread. They shopped at Maria's Italian Delicatessen where they would buy full loaves of crusty Italian bread, cold cuts, and cheese. My sandwiches were two inches thick roughly cut slices of bread filled with mortadella and provolone cheese. The other kids would laugh and poke fun at my lunch. This ridicule would send me into self-imposed isolation just so I could eat the food my mother packed in peace. After school, I would go home and beg my mother to make my sandwiches with regular white bread and bologna or peanut butter. But that was not going to happen. I thought that my life would be forever scarred. It was not until I was in high school and Italian food became a sought-after delicacy that my lunches gained credibility. My friends would barter cafeteria food to get a piece of my unique sandwich. The nightmare was finally over.

It was also in grade six that I made a fateful decision in music class while preparing for the Christmas presentation. As we were practicing our carols the music teacher would stop the singing to remind us again and again that the song was 'LET us adore him' not 'LETTUCE adore him'. When Richard, who was seated in front of me, stood up to sing I strategically positioned a tack on his chair. He struck a high note that was not part of the carol when he sat down. The music teacher and the principal were not amused. The principal summoned my favorite teacher, Mrs. Ross, to join him in a trial and judgement session. The verdict was guilty and punishable by three straps of the belt on my open palm. I would like to say it was a traumatic experience but instead I gained status and credibility not to mention a few laughs with all my friends except Richard. I was now considered a tough guy at school.

However, this type of behavior did not fall in line with the teachings of my Friday night catechism classes. This Catholic training taught by nuns was required because I was attending a Public School. Here we were educated in the virtues of a good Catholic upbringing. It also prepared us for Confession and First Holy Communion. Preparation also meant shopping with my father at the local formal wear shop to purchase the required suit for my First Communion. We had to dress like we were getting married to receive this sacrament. Parents would marvel as their children made their way up the church stairs and down the aisle to the alter looking like mini brides and grooms. They would gush to one another and cameras would snap when their children shuffled by. This would quite likely be the one and only time that they would see their child dressed so impeccably for many years to come. The suit would become a treasured heirloom, never to be worn again.

I am not sure why, but my mother always wanted us to be dressed nicely. Every Sunday, I wore a small brown patterned suit jacket with dress pants and shiny polished shoes to church. I also owned a Perry Como cardigan that I cherished. If we visited relatives, it was an occasion to get dressed up. I think my mother's gentler urban upbringing played a major role in our mandatory dress code.

As young children, Mom would come into our dimly lit rooms every night and kneel next to our beds as she taught us to say our prayers. We would have to make the sign of the cross on our bodies and recite, in Italian, "the Father, the Son and the Holy Spirit," followed by the names of all the people in our lives that we wanted God to watch over. It indoctrinated us to a life of nightly prayer before bed. It was not until we were adults that my mother revealed to us that she would enter our rooms with Dad after we fell asleep to give us kisses. They believed that if they raised us in a stern but loving conservative manner as children, we would not be hampered by emotional weakness as adults. They loved us very much, but they did not want to dote on us or spoil us with affection. This was likely the result of their experiences in a time of struggle when my father said you had to be tough to survive.

In Junior High I experienced the most awkward and unromantic encounter of my budding adolescent life. A friend of mine asked if I would like to go out with Ruth Ann, a rather charming classmate that I secretly had a crush on. She must have sensed my attraction to her and coaxed my friend to approach me. I was one shy and very naïve young lad.

My goofy response was, "Go where?"

Astonished he responded, "What do you mean?"

I answered, "Where does she want to go?"

Well, that romantic exchange, once publicized, sank my love life faster than the Titanic.

Those were also the days of bathroom literature. A trip to any private stall in the boys' washroom was spent reading the latest poetry scribbled on the walls as you sat there doing your business. It was a library filled with raw literature and artwork. Some of it was quite clever and funny, while some was downright graphic and way too descriptive. I always wondered if a good time could really be had if I called Cindy at the number next to her name. Perhaps it was a jilted boyfriend's way to get back at a lost love. I hope Cindy survived the onslaught of phone calls.

There was one literary latrine limerick that caught my attention and managed to embed itself in my memory never to be erased. I always figured it was a guide to any future thoughts I may have had to becoming a bathroom poet. Because of it, I never succumbed to the urge to scribble on bathroom walls. It went like this.

For those who write on shithouse walls,
should roll their shit in little balls
and when they feel they are full of whit,
should eat these little balls of shit.

Well, that did it for me. I could not get the thought of eating little balls of shit out of my head.

As I grew older, the expectation was that I would find employment and make some money. Sneaking coins by forcing a knife through the opening in a can full of coins was not considered earning wages. You could say that my father was more than encouraging me to find a job. One of my first money making enterprises outside of the local fields was delivering newspapers. My route of thirty customers stretched about five miles into the countryside. After school, I would go to the drop off corner and snap the wire containing the papers, fold them and arrange them in my carrier bag. The bag would then fit into the large metal cage mounted on the front of my bike. My route took me out of town along a narrow two-lane country road where I had to shove papers into mailboxes along the way. At one point, I would invariably encounter a German shepherd dog with a raging disdain for paperboys. My stress level skyrocketed every time I had to pass that house. I taught myself several defensive measures for protection. Initially I used my bike as a barrier, but the shepherd would swing around to the other side and growl at me. I even resorted to water pistols and noise makers. The dog never bit me, but I was not interested in giving him the opportunity. Regardless, the dog made my paper route far more difficult than it should have been.

One day as I was riding home from delivering papers, I noticed that the traffic in both directions was quite busy on the narrow, paved country road. Without warning, I suddenly felt myself falling down the face of a sheer cliff. I remember trying to grasp onto the cliff so as not to fall to my death. The next thing I remember was sitting in a stranger's passenger seat with the door open. The gentleman was genuinely concerned and asked if I was alright. I told him I felt fine except for a bit of soreness on my left ass cheek. Then I looked over and there on the grass on the side of the road I could see my red bicycle bent and the seat torn. No one wore a helmet in those days and that may have contributed to my mental disorientation. It finally occurred to me that I had been hit by this man's car and it had sent me flying in the air and knocking me unconscious. His impatience and bad driving skills brought us together that day. He wanted to take me to the hospital, but I insisted on going home. Shortly after the accident the man replaced the broken parts of the bike. My pain eventually subsided, but to this day I still have soft tissue that aches on my left side and back after heavy activity. It turned out that the man who hit me was the owner of the German Shepherd dog.

Near the end of my route, at a fork in the road was Wisey's store. Wisey was an older, heavy-set, gruff middle-aged man. He claimed to have the only hole in the wall store in America. You had to stick your head through a twelve-by-twelve-inch square hole to see inside where the cavernous space held shelves loaded with a variety of products. He took your order through that hole. He would then retrieve and pass your purchase back to you. It was a security feature since he was open almost twenty-four hours a day. It was also necessary since Wisey was the local bootlegger who would sell beer on weekends or after hours at a premium price. Back then, a trip to the Government operated liquor store meant you had to fill out paperwork to buy a bottle of booze. It was much easier but much more expensive to buy from Wisey.

Wisey and I got along well, and he always had colorful stories to tell. He was the first adult that did not treat me like a child, a son, a pupil, or a nephew. He never talked down to me and always seemed interested in what I had to say. He would listen as I recounted the events of my day and any misadventures I may have had. Wisey never said or did anything that was inappropriate. If he was not listening to me, I was spellbound with his stories. He was just one of those people who pass through your young life and leave an impression. Wisey was my first adult friend. The friendship and his guidance were one of the unexpected benefits of my paper route. As a parent, I always tried to take the time to listen to my children and to their friends and not talk down to them. This is what I learned from my friend Wisey.

The newspaper agent that came around once a week to

collect money showed me how to arrange the bills by denomination and always face up with the heads pointing in the same direction. Once I was aware of this little trick, it just felt better when I handed him an organized bundle of money. I think this practice may have also contributed to the OCD that my mother had already instilled in me with the bed making. It is a cross that I bare to this day. I cannot walk past a tilted wall hanging without stopping to straighten and level the picture. My children find it rather humorous and sometimes they deliberately shift pictures and chuckle as I straighten them. They have even been known to move an article out of place and wait for me to notice. Inadvertently, this supervisor gave my children many hours of amusement at my expense.

His standard go to conversation was asking me what I was going to do with all the money I was earning. He would encourage me to spend it wisely. He told me that if I saved my money, someday I could buy a big house. He warned me not to waste it on cars and stereos that are fun to buy but bad investments. I do not think he ever realized how the offhand financial advice that he probably gave to every paperboy under his charge had such an influence on me. I am guessing that it was just conversation to him, but what he did not realize is how much I was really listening and absorbing what he had to say. Through his idle chatter, he inadvertently helped me develop a sensible approach to my finances. He also taught me to be well organized and balanced in my approach to life.

That paper route was also my one and only encounter with a sighting that I can only explain as a UFO. As I placed a paper in a mailbox I happened to glance into the clear sky. High in the heavens, I noticed a brilliant blue light that appeared to be racing to earth at a high rate of speed. As it got closer, it increased in size, stopped abruptly and immediately made a quick turn. As it altered its course, the color changed to red. It then sped off and disappeared into the sky. I could not believe what I had just seen. It was obviously not a plane because I knew how planes moved through the sky. I was both frightened and in awe and wondered if I was imagining things. As much as I wanted to, I never told anyone for fear of being ridiculed. I still cannot explain what I saw but that event convinced me that we are probably not alone in the universe.

Finally, and of most importance at that point in time, the paper route exposed a young, curious, sexually inexperienced boy to a new form of literature. Occasionally, as I delivered my papers something in the ditch would catch my eye. They were forbidden girlie magazines of questionable content. This was the first time that I saw pictures of random naked people. Of course, I would stop and review these treasure troves of artistic expression. They were not your typical air brushed glossy Playboy type magazines. It was page after page of untouched naked people in what looked like nudist camps. I would stop and visually scour the ditch every time that I approached this area. Once I even found a paperback written by Xavier Hollander which was quite risqué at that time. This was my first glimpse into the world of eroticism. My guess is that this area was a dumping ground when someone was ready to move on to the next issue. In those days you could not simply put them in the garbage because the person collecting the refuse might see it. Looking at girlie magazines was not something regular people did and whoever bought those magazines had to cover their tracks. What they did not realize was that they were adding incentive and excitement to a young boy's boring paper route.

Being a paperboy taught me several lessons that would influence my approach to school, to work, and how to live responsibly as an adult. It taught me that people were depending on me and I needed to be punctual and reliable. It taught me that I could not just drop what needed to be done in favor of what I felt like doing. And most importantly, it taught me to be dedicated to whatever it was that I was doing.

The memories of my younger years in my little farm town have never left me. My friends and I endured sleepy, uneventful, seemingly endless summer months trying to amuse ourselves with whatever our collective imaginations could conjure up. As a young child we crawled through the grass looking for four leaf clovers and trekked through forested lots swinging on tree branches. We would shake milkweed pods and watch the seeds float through the air like tiny helicopters. Make believe was our primary source of entertainment. We lived in an idyllic world with little responsibility other than going to school and obeying our parents. We did not have all the toys and gadgets that kids have today, but we did have our imaginations and our friends.

And most importantly for me, I had my large loving Italian family that tried to prepare me for adulthood and any strife that may lay ahead. They knew that one day my siblings and I would emerge from our sheltered existence and enter a world that was not quite as gentle as our little town. They wanted us to be prepared for whatever life had in store for us. Since our strength would no longer be derived from our ever-present family, they felt that we needed to be able to find comfort and direction from what they had ingrained in us as children.

5

THE NEW HOME

When my young newlywed mother and father first moved into the house on Martin Drive, there were only two bedrooms. Both were on the second floor. As the family grew, Dad added another bedroom on the main floor just off the kitchen. My parents slept downstairs and us youngsters, sharing bedrooms, slept upstairs. Living in those cramped quarters for several years resulted in my father's decision to move the family to bigger and better accommodations with more land to spread out and breathe.

Dad bought a lot in a developing subdivision in a small nearby hamlet with a population of 500 residents. This new house would also be surrounded by farms; only this time they were mostly apple orchards. There we embarked on the construction of our new yellow brick ranch style bungalow. With the help of Dad's brother, who also happened to be a mason, the foundation began. Masonry and concrete were two occupations that Italians were well known for. That DNA was handed down through the generations from the ancient Romans who created some of the Empire's most iconic structures. Much of their work was made from concrete, brick, and limestone.

During the building process I would accompany my father and my uncle to the jobsite each weekend where we began by digging the foundation, building the formwork, and then pouring concrete. My father and uncle would lay the block walls and make me work my butt off handing them the blocks. After that came the floor deck. Next came the stud walls, roof, cabling, and plumbing and then onto the final touches like plaster, trim, and painting. This time we had a garage and a concrete driveway. The house had three bedrooms on the main floor and a partially finished and furnished basement for a cost of about 15,000 dollars to build. Of course, most of the labor was free.

My father was an avid smoker and as we travelled to work on the new house dad would usually light up a cigarette. He liked the menthol kind. In the warmer months, it was not too bad since the car windows were wide open, but in the winter months the windows were rolled up and I would almost choke to death on the cigarette smoke. I tried hard to hold my breath at times, but it was still a challenge. Dad never realized what an impact it had on me. The smoke-filled drives made me decide at a young age to never take up the habit. My father eventually gave up smoking which for some strange reason prompted my mother to start. I never did figure that one out. Thankfully, she eventually gave it up too.

The new house would be built in the traditional Italian style with palatial undertones. Mind you, this was no palace, but for us kids it was quite an upgrade. A tour of the final product started with the main floor which had an almost museum quality, fit for velvet rope barriers leading to the living room. It felt like there should be paid guided tours every hour on the hour. My mother would say these rooms were for 'bellezza'. It was not a 'bella figura' to have a messy house. In other words, they were off limits except for dignitaries and celebrities who never seemed to visit. In my mind if it was not for the family, who was all of this for?

The kitchen had new appliances that would seldom be used. The simulated marble counter tops were spotless except for the espresso press and tiny cups. The marble patterned vinyl that my father had special ordered covered the floor. In the dining room under a sparkling chandelier sat a fine rosewood table with perfectly spaced chairs. A knitted tablecloth and a fake bouquet of roses in a sculpted vase adorned the table. The glass display cases were filled with treasures and crystal glassware. French provincial sofas, coffee tables and a wood grained High Fi stereo filled the plush carpeted living room. The only thing missing were sculptures of naked men and women. It was a home fit for a king. Kids need not enter. We the children, the mere occupants, were relegated to the basement where there was a second kitchen and living room. All the appliances and furniture on the lower level were second hand. I believe my OCD and obsession with tidiness was exacerbated by my parents meticulously decorated new home.

Outside was the customary vegetable garden, flower beds and the forty-five-gallon burn drum. Soon grape vines would be creeping up the fence posts as accouterments to my father's urban farmyard. Dad brought his love of gardening and farming to the new house. He even planted a fig tree in an old oak barrel that he cut in half and used as a planter. Each spring that fig tree, which was about five feet high, would be carried outside and each winter it would be covered in plastic and brought back in the garage. Dad would graft apple branches onto pear trees so at harvest time you could pick apples and pears off the same tree.

Mom had an up-to-date version of the outdoor solar powered clothesline with two T shaped steel supports at each end and four plastic coated steel wires running between them. I would share a bedroom with my brother and my two sisters would have their own shared domain. This new home would bring new adventures, new friends, and a new school.

When we moved, I was about to enter grade eight. Being a shy kid, it was difficult to make new friends. I spent many hours sitting on that French provincial couch, staring out the front window towards the orchards and the house across the street. My mother would tell me to go outside and make some friends. That was easy for her to say but it was not an easy thing for me to do. It always took a considerable amount of time and effort for me to cultivate a friendship. Feeling safe, respected, and accepted was a prerequisite before I would let my guard down. Trust was paramount and was expected of anyone that I got close to. Being the first-born son, my mother had ingrained the importance of trust in me. A potential friend had to prove themselves to me and this took time. Once someone earned my trust, they became a friend for life. That is, unless that trust was violated. Then the Old Italian proverb kicked in; "To trust is good, not to trust is better." My father would say "Don't trust anyone, not even yourself."

My self-imposed social isolation probably contributed to the sibling rivalry I had with my sister Hilda, who was named after our neighbor's daughter back on Martin Drive. My dad liked the name. During that period, I would describe my state of mind as angst-ridden. For some crazy reason, I acted out by getting into fights with my sister and pulling her hair. That form of tension release ended one day after I heard a pop as I yanked on a handful of her dark mane. I had pulled a few strands of hair right out of her scalp. This ended the hair pulling but I moved on to punching her in the shoulder. Since I was in the eighth grade by this time, I felt it was a more mature way to fight.

One day, that was also brought to an abrupt end when my mother reached her breaking point. After I punched my sister on the shoulder, she quickly ran away crying and tattled on me. I had been ratted out before but this time something snapped in my mother and she was not going to have any more of this behavior. I could hear Mom rapidly approaching and then saw the look of disgust on her face. Without missing a beat, she landed a 'knuckle sandwich' squarely on my cheek. I had heard the kids at school talk about a knuckle sandwich, but I had never experienced it personally, until then. My head snapped backwards and bumped into the wall. I was dumbfounded, sore and in shock. My mother had just delivered a knockout punch. What was I to do now? My first fist fight was with my mother and I could not fight back.

She looked at me with a determined look like I was about to get an uppercut and said, "How do 'you' like it?"

Well, I did not like it and that ended my boxing career and the bullying of my younger sister. In that moment I knew I had to find a constructive way to relieve my angst. My mother taught me a lesson in a most unconventional way, but it was a lesson well learned and never forgotten.

On cool sunny days, I would lay on the carpeted floor in front of the big picture window. The sun would shine into the room and I would take advantage of the warm comfort that the sun brought. With my eyes shut, I would fantasize about being on some tropical Island with the surf splashing and the sun baking me with warmth. I pictured sandy beaches, umbrella drinks and palm trees swaying in the breeze. It helped to pass the time on those boring weekends when I had little interest in doing anything. At night, however, things were a bit different. Anxiety would kick in. I would lay in bed with fearful thoughts of losing my parents to some tragedy. As the oldest, I would be expected to take charge and that was unnerving. So, each night, I would pray that my parents would live a long life and that all wars would end peacefully.

During those times, I also suffered from painful, crippling migraines. To alleviate the suffering, I would lay on my bed with the curtains drawn. The room needed to be dark so as not to inflame the shooting and debilitating pain in my head. I did a fair amount of reading on the subject and decided to try meditation. I would start by putting myself into a trance like state by slowly relaxing my feet and imagining them sinking into the mattress, then consciously working that sensation up my body until it reached my head. In my mind, I isolated the pain and imagined it was a herd of sheep running loose with the pain throughout my head. I would corral the pain until it was like a ball of hurt that I could manipulate and slowly move around in my head. Finally, and mindfully, I would force the pain out through my ear, nose, or mouth. To my amazement, the technique worked for me. Sometimes it would take hours to accomplish but pain pills did not provide relief. The migraines also led to bouts of depression which prompted me to read books on the topic. I discovered that knowledge helped me overcome some of my challenges. Happily, as I grew older, the migraines ceased, and I was able to get the depression under control.

Across the street from us lived a young couple who had

recently moved in. During the summer months the wife was home most days and would cut the grass and perform the yardwork in her bathing suit. As a young impressionable teen, this got my attention. I was sure that all the aimless staring would send me directly to hell, but I did not care. The reward was worth the risk. It was during this time that I felt compelled to understand what all the hell fire and brimstone was about.

Religion was a topic that left me confused. My parents were devout Catholics and wanted us to follow the doctrine. This puzzled me because church really did not do a great job explaining the religion and why we should believe. When the mass was delivered in Latin, I did not even know what the Priest was saying. I decided I needed to find out on my own. I began my research with the New Testament and started reading it to find out what kind of hell I was destined for. As it turned out, I learned there was no real fire and brimstone, but I discovered the Revelations chapter which was a bit scary. The New Testament was filled with stories of good practices and how to live a decent, honorable, and peaceful life with your fellow man. It told a great story that did seem a bit unbelievable, but it set my mind at ease knowing that I was not doomed and that no one is perfect.

As an adult I read another book called, 'Conversations with God,' that also made sense at the time. I was not totally convinced that the author actually had conversations with God, but some of the insightfulness in that book struck a chord with me. In particular, the understanding that hell does not exist resounded with me. It made complete sense that if you are a Christian and believed that Jesus came to the world to absolve us of our sins through his death, that we are all destined to go to heaven with no questions asked. God would not joke about that, would he? I began to wonder why we were spending so much time convincing each other that good deeds will get us to heaven. In fact, would it not be better for everyone if we just said good deeds will make you a better person and Godlike, thus fulfilling what Christ intended? The book made religion appear to be a source of many philosophies and beliefs that have created problems throughout our history. It made sense to me.

While we are on the topic of religion, it brings me to an incident that although not religious in nature, it highlighted a philosophy taken from religion. Once during my career, I had a mentor who taught me a lot about ethics, respect, good business practices and consequently, a minor but significant bit of religion. George was the vice president of our company. He was a tall, heavy-set gentleman with a charming manner, a killer instinct and a deep voice that would get your attention. I loved travelling with him. He was down to earth, and flying business class was alright with him. On this day, the two of us and one other employee were in a heated negotiation with one of our bigger clients regarding payment of construction claims. The owner kept responding to each of our requests with an example of how badly we had performed. He claimed that we were not justified in our request for additional payments. He repeatedly cited examples of our imperfect product. Suddenly, George reached his breaking point. He was done with the excuses this person was throwing at us. With all six foot three of him firmly planted on the floor and with his hands on the boardroom table, he glared at each of the client representatives.

He spoke calmly but with firm authority and said, "Yes, we made some mistakes, but no one is perfect."

He glared at them and continued, "There was only one

perfect person who ever walked this earth, and we all know what happened to him."

He paused and then said, "I would hate to see anything like that happen to any of you."

At this point we all stood up and walked out of the meeting. His words were profound and stuck with me my entire life. We went back to his car where he had bottles of whiskey in the trunk. He had planned to give them to the client after what he thought would be a successful negotiation. With the less than desirable results, he opened his trunk and handed each of us some fine scotch.

In my first year of high school, I was consumed with trying to fit in by purchasing the latest clothing styles and growing my hair longer. The Beatles had a huge impact on our adolescence. My father and mother were never big fans of long hair or how the younger generation was developing. Prior to the Beatlemania phenomenon, my father would cut my hair either outside or in the basement with my body wrapped in a towel. He had a special pair of scissors and an electric razor, so I would typically sport the parent approved short clean-cut look. Eventually, this homemade haircut was not consistent with my aspirations of popularity. However, my desire for long hair was not keeping with all the expectations of a first-born Italian son. It created quite a scene on one unforgettable day. My father asked if I wanted to go into town with him one Saturday morning. This was nothing out of the ordinary. We still did this quite often, but I had no idea what was to come on this particular day.

We were 'coincidently' walking past his Italian barber shop 'Toni's' when he turned to me and said, "Let's go in and get a haircut."

It dawned on me that I was in the midst of an ambush. I could feel the anxiety building inside me. My father had cleverly orchestrated this encounter and we were now in the grips of a standoff.

"No way Dad," I answered.

"What do you mean?" he responded. "Let's get that haircut."

Our voices carried as we both turned up the volume. I knew that by giving in my head would look like I had just signed up for the marines. He kept denying the potential severity of Toni's haircut. All I could envision was my popularity being driven into the ground like a heat seeking torpedo. The five-minute exchange between the two of us felt like an hour. I was determined to save the locks of black wavy hair that hung past my ears. In my opinion, the hair along with my bell bottom pants, Nehru shirts and blue suede shoes were what defined me. Thankfully, my father grudgingly relented, and we drove home in dead silence. As much as I respected my father and quite often conceded to the oldest Italian in the family rationale, this was a skirmish I was not willing to lose. As uncomfortable as it was, I had to draw my line in the sand. This was one issue where there was no compromise to be had.

Around that time, my mother noticed that my younger brother was starting to show signs of 'hippy' hair. While my dad was at work, she asked me to give my brother a haircut. This was uncharted territory for me. I had never cut hair before, but it did not look that difficult to me at the time. Judging by the massacre I performed on my poor brother's head, I knew barbering was not my calling. I felt shear (pun intended) pity for him. He had more terraces on his head than a hillside rice farm. Thankfully when my father got home, he turned that cow's ear into a silk purse.

Around that time my father's sister, Aunt Vittoria and her husband Uncle Joe started their own small hobby farm.

They grew vegetables and sold them at their roadside stand. This stand ran on the honor system. Cars would stop and the occupants would pick out vegetables and then place their money in a jar that was left on the counter. My uncle Joe had a full-time job at the factory in addition to tending to his small farm. When I was a teenager, I would volunteer my weekends to help them plant their crops. It was there that I learned to drive his tractor as we planted lettuce and tomatoes. After a morning of hard, dirty work tending to the crops, my aunt would serve lunch at the outdoor table under a shade tree. Working on his farm conjured up images of what I thought days in the old country must have been like.

As a reward, my uncle gave me an old light green 1958 Chevy that he had parked behind his shed. He was not sure why, but it would not run so I had the car towed home. What a stroke of luck! It was not fancy or luxurious, but I was proud to have a car. I stored it in the empty lot next door to our house that happened to be owned by my dad's brother. Uncle Clem gave me the thumbs up to turn it into my own personal dirt track. Visions of NASCAR fame rolled through my mind. Guys like Richard Petti and Cale Yarborough were my racing idols and I pretended that I was making my fledgling debut. Did I mention that youthful inspiration can create phenomenal fantasies of grandeur?

Convinced that this '58 Chevy would be my ticket to fame, I tried to get it into running condition. I removed the head covers and found that the push rods were all bent. After straightening the rods and replacing the rocker covers, I held my breath and cranked her over. It took a few tries, and the car eventually started and ran fine after that. That Chevy just sat in the empty lot except for when I would go next door and race around in circles. My only competition was myself and I always crossed the finish line in first place. I did not have my driver's license yet, but I thought all this practice would help me pass the test.

A few years later, after I almost failed my driver's test with a bad parallel parking attempt, dad bought me a 1965 dark blue Ford Falcon with a manual on the column shift. It was not my first choice, but I was happy to own four legal wheels. It was in this car that I got my first ticket. I was charged with unnecessary noise. You might assume it was because of a loud muffler but that was not the case. After an evening of beer drinking, rock and roll and debonair theatre at the Lakeside bar it was sheer bad luck that I turned out of an A&W too aggressively and allegedly chirped the front tires. At least that is what the officer wrote me up for. It was annoying because I knew it was really my drinking buddy who burned out as he left the A&W just ahead of me in his customized Pinto. As luck would have it, the officer saw me leave and the chase was on.

Flashing lights chased me down the road to the restaurant where my band of buddies and I always met up after a night of underage drinking. I had a few drinks earlier that evening and I was concerned about getting busted. When the policeman caught up with me and placed me in his vehicle, I made sure that I faced the passenger window to avoid breathing in his direction. He continued to write me up without asking for an explanation or at the very least, an excuse. Throughout this ordeal, my loyal and supportive friends were watching from inside the restaurant and were having a good laugh. Since this was my first ticket ever, I asked the officer what I should do with it. He explained that I could just pay the one hundred and fifty dollars or go to court and dispute it. MY TICKET WAS GOING TO

COST ONE HUNDRED AND FIFTY DOLLARS? My father was going to kill me!

Sure enough Dad was not amused when I explained my predicament the next morning. I approached him while he was shaving. His first question was how could I squeal the tires on a 1965 Ford Falcon? I did my best to explain the situation. After some arduous back and forth we agreed our best option was to go to court and fight the ticket. One hundred and fifty bucks was a lot of money. I began reading articles about the finer details of fighting a traffic violation. My plan was ready and my script was complete. I decided my best defense would be that the cop ambushed me and he nailed the wrong guy. Dad took the day off from his job and made the forty-five-minute drive to the city courthouse with me that morning. We sat in the court room waiting to be called. There were about a dozen other people waiting to have their cases heard. After two cases where completed, I heard the bailiff call out my name. I made my way to the front and stood before the judge looking up to where he sat behind a monster sized desk. I could feel the anxiety build in every limb of my body.

He read the charge out and asked, "How do you plea?"

I replied, "Not guilty Sir."

He then called out for the police officer. I will never forget Officer Ostrander's name. The courtroom was quiet. There was no response. The judge called out once more. There was silence once again.

The judge then turned to the bailiff. "Go out into the hall and summon Officer Ostrander."

I could hear the bailiff yelling his name in the hall and in my naïve mind I was wondering why he needs to be so loud. I did not realize that no response would be a good thing for me. Apparently the officer never materialized because the bailiff returned to the courtroom minus the policeman.

The judge, still looking down at the ticket said, "Case dismissed."

In my anxiety, I missed that little tidbit of information. I did not move and after a minute the judge looked at me and said, "You can go."

I was totally shocked. This is it? Yes, that was it. My dad and I left with a sense of accomplishment. We were off to Burger King for a victory celebration. In retrospect, I suspect the officer avoided that court case on purpose because maybe he just wanted to teach me a lesson. After all, this was the 1970s.

Guys and their cars were an especially bad mix when more than two occupants were involved. We had this crazy friend named Alfred who owned a Rambler. One of his favorite driving terror tactics that would scare the living hell out of you if you rode with him, involved another vehicle driven by his brother. Anytime they encountered each other on a quiet street going in opposite directions they would switch lanes, pass each other, and then get back into their proper lanes. After that we all needed a change of underwear. And that was not his worst maneuver. That was yet to come.

One time we were behind another carload of guys driving a Chevy and they were going a bit too slow for Alfred. He rode their bumper until it was safe to pass. As we sped by, we all shot the one finger salute to express our sentiments. That got them moving a bit faster. They sped up so much that they were now on our bumper. It was getting serious. Alfred put the pedal to the metal and the chase was on. We shot down the country road until we neared a farm laneway. He hit the brakes hard and turned up a single lane dirt road that would take us through an apple orchard. We ripped through those trees kicking up so much dust that we could not see if the car was still behind us. No sooner were we out of the orchard and in the clear when we realized that right in front of us was the incline of a steep hill that appeared to have a set of railroad tracks on its crest. The four of us wailed in unison. We ascended the hill without any problem. On the way down the wheels left the ground and I felt the force of gravity disappear. We were airborne. The car landed a four-wheel slam, but Alfred still kept his foot on the accelerator. Eventually when we were sure that we had lost our predators we stopped and checked the vehicle for damage. The car was perfectly intact and we were happy to still be alive.

6

HIGH SCHOOL

In my senior year of high school, my best friend Brian and I were both asked to run for student council president. The principal encouraged us to enter the race because the only other candidate was a known marijuana user, and this would not go over well with the school staff. The principal was afraid the school would turn into a nation of pot heads. We were not sure why he chose us but we were flattered by his stamp of approval. He was insistent that one of us run. We pondered the options and discussed the possibilities. Brian graciously decided to decline the offer and we began planning my campaign.

We built the campaign around a nonsensical and fun theme. My team and I would think of ways to make the campaign enjoyable and memorable but still convey a serious message. We had fun making buttons with silly statements like 'Bob kisses babies' or 'Bob Mafia will make you an offer you can't refuse'. Morning public address announcements were produced using comical characters. At one point, we found an old tire and wrote on it 'You won't get tired of Bob'. We brought it into the school and randomly rolled the tire around the halls until one day someone bowled over Mrs. Brown, the little old English teacher. I was summoned to the Principal's office and was asked to remove the old tire from the premises.

On Election Day, four of my buddies and I came up with a scheme that we were sure would solidify my popularity. Our friend Wally had wealthy parents who owned a long black Lincoln Continental. The five of us would dress up like sinister secret service agents. We planned to arrive in the Lincoln when the school parking lot was full of students. My four bodyguards would exit the vehicle and then I would emerge all decked out in a black suit, hat, dark sunglasses, and a rose in my lapel. We would walk the halls and go from class to class in formation, with me in the middle. This attracted quite a bit of attention as we made our way through the school. It was lighthearted and was positively received by most students. Even the teachers thought it was funny although I am not sure this approach would be kindly received in today's schools.

Between Math and English class, we came upon one well known, but somewhat nerdy student who had a streak of stubbornness. Most of the students recognized our lighthearted attempt at humor and would clear a path as we approached. When we came close to him, he showed no signs of moving aside as everyone else had done. He chose to stand his ground. The five of us came to a stop and my friend Joe asked him to step away. Even though Joe was a big fellow, the student declined his request. None of us knew that Joe had a starter pistol until he quickly drew it out of his pocket, aimed, and fired at the defiant student. We were shocked when the pistol gave off a blast that not only scared us, but sent the resistant student reeling as if he was hit by a bullet. He fell back with a look of terror on his face and reached to find the wound. Of course, there was no wound. We laughed hysterically when we all realized what had happened. That is, except for the unwitting victim. Embarrassed, he walked away grumbling under his breath. Later that day I was voted in as class president by an overwhelming majority. I know that today this would be viewed as unacceptable and probably illegal, but it just shows you how innocent the times were.

My friend, Joe, was obsessed with streaking. He just liked being naked. He was a stocky fellow with a full head of bushy hair and a beard. Even his body was covered in hair. He would go into the boy's washroom, strip himself naked and then run through the halls during class time when most students were in class. To see it, you needed to know about his plan, or you would likely miss the exhibition. One fateful day as he was running through the halls in his birthday suit, bunny ears and sandals, he turned a corner and upon noticing a teacher he slid out of control on the terrazzo floor knocking her to the ground. This was his undoing. Now that his secret was common knowledge, he earned a reputation, as well as a good talking to and a detention. Joe, however, did not stop his freewheeling nudity. He continued his streaking escapades but never again at school. After all, this was the 1970s and streaking was common practice.

Joe and I loved football and we were big fans of the NFL. We cheered our rival teams when his Steelers were led by Terry Bradshaw and my Vikings were led by Fran Tarkenton. We also played on the school football team. His size made him an effective tackle while I played defensive safety. A part of our practice was running the trails behind the school. The land around our school was mostly bush and farms. One day during our routine run, we veered a bit off course and discovered a crop of wild marijuana. At least we thought it was wild. In hindsight, it could easily have been someone's hidden crop. In any case we knew it was illegal. After school, we went back to the illicit crop and pulled leaves off the plants planning to dry them and then smoke them. At that time, we did not realize it was the buds that delivered the THC. Through sheer ignorance, we left the best part of the plant behind and erroneously concluded that marijuana was not all that it was cracked up to be. It was many years later that we finally realized our mistake.

Joe and I became wandering adventurers. The need to expand our horizons during high school prompted us to branch out from our little enclave and hitch hike to the big city for a weekend of anticipated insanity. The city was a good five-hour drive away. This meant that we had to be on the road early with our thumbs positioned to hitch a free ride. It would take most of the day to get there. Our first ride was with a travelling drummer who was in bad need of some shuteye. He was a very trusting fellow because he allowed me to drive his vehicle to his destination. Unable to get another ride to take us the rest of the way to the city, we were forced to walk to the nearest town and grab a bus from there.

As luck would have it, we were blessed with a drunken passenger who threatened to kill everyone on the bus. It turned an uneventful and relatively quiet ride into a fearsome nightmare. We sat right behind him. I took my jacket off and rolled it up between my fists. Should he stand up, I would be ready to shut him down. After a few minutes of the intoxicated terrorist's threats the driver finally pulled the bus over, approached him and gave him a strong warning that if he said one more word he would be left at the side of the highway. He capitulated and eventually fell asleep. We pulled into the bus station and we all filed out of the bus unharmed. When I think about the trip, it reminds me of that scene in the comedy 'Airplane' where everyone takes turns smacking the one whining passenger. I sometimes wonder if the person that wrote that scene was a passenger on our bus.

Upon arrival in the brightly lit city, we headed for the first bar we could find. It was an Irish pub, and we were the only people there. After a beer and some idol conversation, we decided to take a joy ride on the subway before we retired for the night. We rode the train for over an hour from one end of the city to the other. When we finally returned to our cheap room, which by the way came complete with a standard neon flashing sign outside our window, we passed out for the night. The next morning, I awoke and went straight to the small sink and mirror to splash some cold water on my face. The sink and the two beds were the only furniture or amenities in the room. The toilets were down the hall. I squinted into the mirror and to my horror I saw two dark vertical black lines going down each side of my face. Horrified, I asked Joe where the lines came from.

He looked at me and said, "Don't you remember? The subway doors closed right when you were standing in the doorway to get on."

"What?" I replied incredulously. "You mean I was walking around town last night with these lines on my face?"

He confirmed that I was. My bubble was burst. I thought that the long looks the girls were giving me the previous night meant they thought I was good looking. And Joe being the loyal friend that he was, did not mention that I looked like a fool.

After cleaning up and getting primed for a full day of adventure we decided to go for a swim at the YMCA. We arrived to see a notice that read 'All men must swim in the nude'. Thinking it was a joke, we walked into the swim area and there before us were all these old guys swimming buck naked. We looked at each other and that is when we decided to turn around and find some alternative form of entertainment. The city was filled with high and low-end attractions. With our limited finances low-end and free attractions were all that we could afford. The weekend ended uneventfully and after another long day of hitchhiking we arrived at home intact. That trip proved to be one of the more exciting points of our high school careers.

Back at home Joe, Brian and I would hang out and look for different ways to amuse ourselves. Since we were underage, we would try to get into bars by burning cork and smearing the black carbon onto our faces to create a fake five o'clock shadow. To have any chance of success the bar had to be very dark. Despite our efforts, this usually failed. Plan B was to score some booze through older school acquaintances. This usually worked. Our favorite was Old Sailor wine that sold for a dollar a bottle. It was known as 'screech,' because that was the sound you made after you drank it.

When we were running low on cash, homemade wine and cheese pizza was our go to. We would raid my uncle's wine cellar and free a bottle from his wine racks. Pizza was the food of choice and the cheapest meal we could get. We had a favorite pizza joint, where, if we pooled our money, we were able to buy a coveted cheese pizza. One time I emerged from the restaurant holding the box like it was an attaché case. As I approached the car Joe was screaming at me to hold the box flat. It was only then that it dawned on me what I had done. I realized my carryout method was not too clever, but it seemed like a good idea at the time. The pizza now looked like lasagna, but it still tasted great washed down with a beer. In our underage yet to be fully developed brains and palates, beer or wine could make anything look and taste good.

I met my first girlfriend in my remote little community. This romance created some strained and difficult exchanges with my parents. Young infatuation typically leads to tough lessons in life and love. I recall many late moonlight filled nights creeping quietly out of the house to rendezvous with my new emotional addiction. One night after my clandestine encounter, I returned home in the wee hours of the morning to find my father sitting at the kitchen table. Damn! I was busted. That father and son session did not go well. He was adamant that I would not sneak out of the house again and I was hell bent on not stopping.

The first and only time I tried running away from home happened during that period. My parents were not fond of the girl that I was madly infatuated with and totally attached to. Young love and all the emotion attached to it was overtaking logic and making me act out in ways I would not normally behave. Today I look back on that point in time and just shake my head. I left home for just one weekend, but it left bad feelings between me and my parents for quite some time. Trust was lost and their disappointment, even though it was unspoken, was palpable for quite some time. The only plus side of my misguided adventure was that it taught me a valuable lesson that I tapped into as a parent. Spending nights outside curled up in a blanket was not as comfortable as my own warm bed.

I had officially graduated from a young boy to a girl-crazy adolescent. My relationship with this girl also led to my first brawl. Apparently, her previous boyfriend did not like me hanging out with her, so he unleashed one of his brutish friends on me. Walking home from school one day it felt like someone was following me. Sure enough, it was an ambush. Four local guys led by her ex-boyfriend caught up with me and surrounded me pretending they were my friends. The designated enforcer then stepped closer and looked me in the eye while he cocked his arm back ready to fire the first volley with his fist. My instincts and wrestling training kicked in. I quickly had him pinned to the ground in a full nelson while he struggled to get free. At that point, my only concern was how do I get away now that I had him pinned. He was like a spitting mad honey badger threatening me with death. I quickly recalculated my strategy, released him, and made a speedy escape, running like my life depended on it. This was where my cross-country training and stamina kicked in. I would live to fight another day, but hopefully I would not have to. After that day, I was constantly on the lookout for potential threats.

My first love also gave me my second death defying experience with water. This time there was no lifeguard on duty to save me. My girlfriend had convinced me to skip school one unusually warm spring day and hang out at the beach. The secluded beach happened to be about a mile down the road from my house. You had to take a long set of stairs down a cliff to the sandy beach and water below. Once there, we spread out a blanket and soaked up some sun.

After a few minutes, she turned to me and said, "Hey, you know there is a rock out there about one hundred feet from shore in about a foot of water that you can stand on."

The water was deep all around the rock and well over our heads, so I was a bit apprehensive. She did not know that I could not swim. She said she knew the location of the rock by lining up some land features which would point us to its location. I was still not convinced.

Totally embarrassed I said, "I can't swim." She looked around and found a good-sized log lying on the beach.

"I have an idea!" she said.

Trepidation pulsed through my veins, but so did testosterone and I did not want to appear weak to my girlfriend. We dragged the log over and dropped it into the water to see if it would float. I pushed it out a few feet and held on to it as the water got deeper. Eventually, I could not feel the bottom of the lake anymore. She pulled the log and swam towards the rock, while I held on and paddled. Sure enough we found the rock and there we stood. Once we arrived the only thing to do was head back to shore.

It was quite a thrill to be standing and looking all around with nothing but deep water surrounding me. In that moment, I completely forgot about the log that brought me there. The rock was large enough for two people and nothing else. It was then that my girlfriend accidently bumped me, and I fell into the deep water. In full panic mode, I thrashed about fearing it was all over for me. Goodbye world. I do not remember seeing my life flash before me because I was too focused on trying to stay alive. Unexplainedly, I raised one arm into the air and in that instant I could feel the log on the palm of my hand. Pulling myself up I caught my breath and tried to remember what had happened.

I was gripped with tension and shaking with fear as I yelled to her, "Why did you push me off?"

"It was an accident! I did not mean to do that. I am so sorry," she insisted. She kept repeating it was unintentional and continued apologizing over and over again. Paranoia set in. Who knows, maybe her ex-boyfriend had plotted with her? The perceived conspiracy would have made a great episode of Crime Discovery. The answer was actually far simpler and less sinister. She had the presence of mind to push the log over to me as I was thrashing in the water. Rather than trying to kill me, she saved my life. Maybe it was not part of a plot to kill me after all.

In grade eleven, long after that relationship faded, a female classmate who was apparently more mature than the rest of us sat right behind me in class. Cathy was an attractive girl with long dark hair who enjoyed a good laugh and was easy to like. For some reason, she took a special liking to me as I did to her. We always had fun during class. One afternoon she challenged me to skip class and spend the rest of the day with her. At first, I was a bit apprehensive. I was not well practiced in the habit of ditching school.

I relented and the rest of the day we were AWOL. She wanted to spend time at her house where to my astonishment I learned she was engaged to be married. She explained that she wanted to have her last and final fling before her wedding day. I was flattered to be her chosen one. However, all she wanted to do was kiss, grind, and hug. We did that a few times and we were able to stay friends after that. She got married, became a cashier at the grocery store and I assume had a wonderful life. Every time I went to that store, I would make a point to stop and talk to her. I always wondered if she remembered that day.

The only time there was intrigue in that sleepy little town, the story became a legend. One block away from the four corners was a popular bar that filled up with a wide range of patrons every night. It was the place to be. The music was rock and roll and live bands would play on weekend nights. It was so popular that it eventually caught the attention of the local motorcycle gang. The only downside with the gang's frequent presence was that the younger crowd started to take their business elsewhere. The bar started to take on a biker reputation and the club owner was not happy with that. The rumor in town was that the owner had connections if you know what I mean.

That sunny afternoon, the usual rows of motorcycles were parked outside the hotel. Without fanfare, six black limousines pulled up. A dozen well-dressed men looking agitated yet focused stepped out of the vehicle. They stood for a second, adjusted their suits, did a visual scope, and then filed in through the front entrance. What happened next is based on pure speculation. The rough looking leathered bikers left the establishment with blood dripping from several of their bearded faces. Motorcycles revved up and the gang rode off. Shortly afterwards the suited strangers emerged, got back into the waiting limos, and drove away. It all took place within a half hour. The club returned to a lively hot spot like nothing ever happened and the bikers never returned.

We spent a couple more high-school years as relatively carefree teenagers before we parted ways and moved on to the next phase of our lives. We managed to stay out of trouble and we were all accepted by the University or College of our choice. Little did we know that the small town we were so eager to leave was the place that we would fondly remember as we grew older. We sometimes had the worst of times but overall, they were the best and most influential times of our lives. It was not until we ventured out of our rarified existence that we realized how fortunate we were to grow up in the protective cocoons of our families and our little town.

7

GROWING OLDER

A fter leaving for college, the first apartment I rented had a swimming pool that no one ever seemed to use. Having managed to steer clear of a potential watery death for several years, it was at this time that I finally decided to confront my fear. Growing up in a town situated on a peninsula surrounded by water, I should have learned to swim many years ago. After all, I had almost drowned twice. Surely, I was the only person in the county that did not know how to swim. Each day after class I would get into that pool and dog paddle lengths until I learned to swim and float without panicking. It was one of the best things I ever did. Later as a parent, I made sure my children were accomplished swimmers before they started school. I did not want them to experience the terror, the embarrassment and ridicule that I endured as a child.

During my post-secondary years, this country boy experienced some rather interesting city events. It introduced me to all walks of life and taught me how much the world outside of my small town lived. My apartment was in something of a 'fringe' neighborhood. Standing on the balcony and looking down from my ninth-floor apartment, I was amazed at how many eligible young women seemed to live in my neighborhood. The truth revealed itself one day when I noticed a fashionably dressed woman leaning into a car window. Initially, I presumed she was having a chat with the driver. Eventually, the passenger door opened and she hopped in. It finally dawned on me why there were so many women plying the concrete paths in my neighborhood. It seemed ironic because the headquarters of a large and popular religious movement was next door to my building. Up until this point, in my naïve mind I just thought that it would be easy to get a date. This was my first introduction to how different city life would be.

Across the street was a towering glass clad apartment building. In the unit almost directly across from me lived a young woman who I imagine shared my friend Joe's clothing is optional rule. I could not decide whether pulling her drapes shut was not a priority or whether she was an exhibitionist and liked to be on display. In my eyes she had nothing to fear by being on view. From my distant perch, she looked perfect. Everything about her looked absolutely fine to me. This country boy was gaining volumes of education in big city social behavior.

One weekend in the early fall, my parents decided it was time to visit me at university and see what I was up to. The three of us sat in my apartment as I brought them up to date on my life in the city. We were chatting in the living room when my father decided to go out on the balcony and look at the sparkling city lights. My mother and I stayed inside and continued our conversation.

After an extended period of time, Mom asked, "What is your father doing out there?"

In the back of my mind, I had my suspicions. "I'm not

sure. He's probably enjoying the view." I did not completely lie.

That is when he reappeared and asked, "Bob, do you have a pair of binoculars?"

"Sorry, dad, I don't." Now that was a complete lie.

My apartment was a ten-minute walk to the college. Early one morning as I was making my way to class, I noticed a black cloud of smoke rising above the downtown buildings. I realized that this cannot be a good thing in the middle of the city. I picked up my pace, walked past numerous stores and turned the corner. There in front of me was a yellow taxicab engulfed in flames. There did not appear to be anyone inside. I wondered if this was the result of a fare that did not want to pay. Did they light up the cab as a diversion while they ran off? My mind momentarily lapsed to my childhood cops and robbers' days. No one seemed too concerned. The firemen and police had not yet arrived at the scene. There were only three other onlookers watching the flames as they grew higher. I assumed one was the cabdriver. It must have just happened, and I was witnessing breaking news.

Slowly, I walked up to one of the bystanders and asked, "What happened here?" The fellow did not seem to have an answer. He shook his head and gave a bit of a grunt. It was then that I noticed a cop walking towards us. He stopped and stood on the other side of the fellow I was just talking to.

He asked the young man, "How long have you been out?" That is when I realized it was time to keep moving. There was nothing to see here. I continued my walk to class just as the fire trucks with their sirens wailing pulled up.

During my second year of university, I shared a flat with a school mate. It was the cheapest apartment we could find.

Unfortunately, it was in a part of town I referred to as West Side Story. The day before class started, I had returned to the city to prepare the second story flat that would be our home base for that term. A bus would take me directly from the train station to the apartment. Although it was a sketchy neighborhood, logistically it was perfect.

As I neared the flat, I noticed an older gentleman sifting through charred furniture on the front lawn of the old two-story Victorian style home. Once I approached him it became clear that he was the landlord. He introduced himself and with a bit of conversation I realized that he was Alex Trebek's father. Yes, that Alex Trebek. He told me that the first-floor occupant had fallen asleep while smoking and that I should go upstairs and assess the second-floor apartment's damage. Fortunately, it did not have serious fire damage except that the kitchen and bathroom were now black and covered with soot. For obvious reasons, we cleaned up the bathroom the best that we were able to but left the kitchen for the insurance people to clean. Apparently, they were not in a hurry to get the job done. It took weeks for the kitchen to be restored to the point where it was usable again. During that time, our diet was mostly submarine sandwiches and Kentucky Fried Chicken. But we did not mind. It went well with our beer.

My roommate Joe, who was not related to my friend from high school, shared his love of beer. This worked out well because we were able to stack the empty cases and use them as couches and tables. My contribution to the furnishings was a stereo system with a floating turn table, a receiver and an amplifier connected to a couple of four-foot-high speakers filled with tweeters, woofers, sub woofers and a base. We thought we had it all.

It did not take long to figure out that we were in a rough

part of the city. More than once I would be awakened in the middle of the night by some sort of drama unfolding below. I would slowly creep to my bedroom window and carefully peer from the dark room through a crack in the drapes. One night I watched a live version of West Side Story complete with chains and bats. Only this time the gang violence was real. Another night, I heard the familiar sound of a squeaking brake that I routinely heard when a cab stopped out front. This was followed by the sound of a hand-held radio conversation. I got in position behind the curtains. Below a dozen police cars filled the street. I heard an officer say that one of the suspects was wearing a leather jacket. That is when I shut the curtains fearing they would think it was me. After a while this seemed commonplace and became less noteworthy. I realized that walking through the neighborhood at night was either an act of bravery or just sheer stupidity. From that time on, I ventured out after dark only if it was unavoidable.

Trying to find something to occupy myself outside of school, I trained and signed up to be a ski patroller. This would give me a reason to hit the slopes during the long winters and it would offset the cost. Turning my love of skiing into a job gave me free access to the slope I was assigned to patrol. After a two-month training period, I was given my gear and apparel and was certified ready to go. My weekends outdoors were a break from the many hours of assignments and class time and it allowed me to escape the lunacy of the neighborhood. It gave me an opportunity to meet many different and sometimes interesting people. The hills I patrolled where not the size of a slope in Stowe or Lake Tahoe, but it was heaven to me.

Remarkably, only one embarrassing situation marked my tenure. The ride up the mountain was quite short and relatively quick. If there was another skier in the chair, it usually resulted in idle conversation. Such was not the case on this day. I quickly got into a deep conversation with the other person on the lift. We were so engrossed in our discussion neither one of us realized it was time to dismount. As the chair swung around past the discharge point, we quickly realized that we were headed back down. Simultaneously, we both jumped from the chair. The unfortunate and embarrassing outcome was that a Ski Patroller trained to keep the slopes safe landed on top of a skier in the snow. Thinking I may have injured the person I was tasked to keep safe, I imagined the headline, 'Ski Patroller Crushes Skier'. Thankfully, there were no injuries, and I was more than happy to escort my new friend to the bottom of the hill for a hot beverage and a sandwich.

On another occasion, I was on a school ski trip where my classmates' skiing skills ranged from expert to "you want me to go down that?" We had one young girl in our group named Sheryl who had never been on skis. Once we arrived at the top of the slope, those of us who were experienced tried to teach her how to snowplow. This was an elementary, basic technique for a novice skier. It would give her the ability to slow down and stop if she picked up too much speed and things got out of control. As she pushed off, she went down the hill straight as an arrow at full speed. Thankfully, we were on the bunny hill, so her speed was limited, but that did not stop her from racing down the slope straight towards the full parking lot. We were all shouting for her to fall to one side. Unfortunately, that did not happen. She was too terrified to do anything. Like a bullet she shot into the parking lot. Somehow, she made it past several rows of cars without hitting one. A roar of applause and cheers followed. Even though we knew it was luck we told her that it took great skill to miss the parked vehicles. As instructors, we failed miserably.

Paying for university meant I had to work summers back home. Since I grew up in a farming community, it was easy to find jobs in the agriculture sector with the help of my mother and my uncles. I drove stake trucks, picking up produce and sometimes smashing barn doors due to my poor backup skills. I also worked in warehouses loading produce onto transports and rail cars which would then be shipped to faraway markets. Eventually I worked my way up to becoming a government inspector of fruits and vegetables. It paid very well and made a big dent in my tuition. The hard work was all worth it. My parents had never finished school and they insisted that I get an education. I knew they were proud of me.

My passion, however, was art. I enjoyed drawing and wanted to become an architect. This aspiration was dashed the day I arrived for an interview at one of the well-known schools of architecture. After comparing our portfolios, I realized I did not have the artistic talent to become the next Frank Lloyd Wright. I changed my focus and entered a university that taught me the next best thing, managing construction. It became my life.

However, after a few years of working as a construction coordinator, disillusionment started to set in. Whether it was due to a midlife crisis or just the need to leave some sort of mark on the world, I succumbed to this like many others do at some point in their lives. It is a nagging feeling that you need to do something epic whether it makes sense or not. Looking for answers, I sometimes tempted myself with adventurous options. Seeking spiritual guidance, I once drove two hours to listen to Billy Graham during one of his crusades. It was inspiring but it did not help me understand what I needed to do. I read books *like Future Shock, Small is Beautiful* and even survival guides. The need to accomplish something beyond what I perceived as my daily never ending, repetitive drudgery kept pushing me to go further. That epic moment finally came in the form of an adventure that in the end would help me temper my aspirations.

A college friend and I fell in love with the idea of buying a resort property and living on a remote northern lake. This would allow us to say goodbye to city life and our nine to five daily grind. We spent months searching property after property and finally settled on a picturesque lodge that boasted fine dining and seven cottages. Financing this venture was going to be a challenge. Banks turned us down and government funding failed to materialize. I can still hear the voice of one particular agent saying, "There are two types of ships to stay off of, sinking ships and partnerships." We laughed and assured him that we were good friends, and we would strive to make it work. After all, we were pursuing our dreams. We kept searching for money and we finally managed to find a venture capital group to finance the mortgage. Unfortunately, the previous banker's warning turned out to be so true.

By this time, I was married and had children. The next big step was to sell our homes, pack up our wives and toddler children, our belongings and move to what we thought would be paradise. Looking back, that decision seems so radical and crazy now. The property named 'The Norseman' was ideal. It was a large two-story clapboard main lodge housing a fine dining restaurant with a huge deck and two spacious second story apartments. It also had seven quaint cottages facing the small lake. Just down the road from us at another resort a bright and talented singer was making her debut as an entertainer. Shania Twain was just starting her singing career and her publicist stopped in one day to promote her. He met with my business partner and left him a promotional tape of Shania's performance. As we all know, she went on to become a superstar. We were also visited by local celebrities who enjoyed the cuisine and atmosphere. Despite all the wonderful things that happened, it only took one summer and a fall season to turn our dream into a nightmare.

Long hours, exhausting work, sleepless nights, endless repairs, maintenance, and unrest amongst the partners turned our fantasy into the proverbial nightmare. It was shortly after that first fall when the summer trade had dwindled that I went back to my old job just to make ends meet. While I was away working, my partners tirelessly continued to operate the struggling business. Each year brought more loss and just when it all seemed hopeless two years later, we managed to escape bankruptcy through the sale of the lodge. That ended our perfect dream gone sour. Now it was someone else's problem. Our two years of stress and unbearable worry took its toll on everyone. If it were not for the soothing escapism of Jimmy Buffett, I surely would have lost it. For some crazy reason, those tropical tunes gave me hope and perspective. The song 'Pirate Looks at Forty' resonated with me. The lyrics, 'I made enough money to buy Miami, but I pissed it away so fast' spoke to me. We lost a bit of money, but we survived. Looking back, I now refer to this period as my relatively cheap education in a business partnership. Lessons from that failure would come in handy later in life.

Now that I was back at work, I focused on my career which once again flourished. Insanity has been defined as doing the same thing again and again hoping for a different result. I can attest to that. Time may heal all wounds, but I have come to conclude that insanity just lays dormant in the back of your mind. As it turned out, I had not completely learned my lesson.

After fifteen years of licking my wounds, I once again partnered in a renovation that resulted in a first-class boutique restaurant and hotel. It took several years to complete the renovation of the old mansion and to bring it back to its Victorian 1885 era glory. The architectural history and vintage features pulled me into the venture. The results were exquisite due to the top-quality workmanship. However, due to our inability to manage and market the somewhat remote location, it too was unprofitable.

Thankfully, my prior experience taught me to limit my exposure. At this time, I was also involved in a commercial plaza partnership. Whether it was due to experience or simply good fortune, that venture was exceedingly successful. The partners gelled fabulously. After ten years of operation and an eventual sale, it turned a major profit far exceeding any of our expectations. It more than made up for all the previous losses. It was then that I decided to permanently get out of partnership ventures while I was still ahead and instead focus on my career. That nagging feeling of doing something epic had finally run its course. In retrospect, all was not lost in the business failures that I had. It taught me that failure is just one step to success. If you never learn to deal with failure, you will never genuinely appreciate success.

8

THE SOBERING REALITY

A few days have now passed since my mother's dramatic phone call and I find myself once again heading back to my hometown. It has been almost a year since Dad was admitted to the small community hospital which sits on the edge of town. Pulling into the parking lot I looked at the Volkswagen dealership across the street and thought of happier and more carefree times. During my high school years, I had a friend that was related to the owner. I do not know if it was due to blind trust or sheer insanity, but the owner recruited my friends and me to drive new cars home from the big city five hours away. Six of us jumped at this opportunity. Besides having a chance to drive a brand-new VW beetle, it was an opportunity to get out of town.

The owner picked us up early one November morning. Five hours later we selected our vehicles at the compound and started the long trek back to town. We were like a swarm of colorful bees as we drove down the highway in single file through an unexpected snowfall. The lead car pulled into a rest stop and one by one we followed it into the mostly empty snow-covered parking lot. We could not resist the temptation to do some spinning donuts in the slippery snow. Even now I smile as I think of the six Volkswagens spinning around in the parking lot. The owner was having a minor fit watching us perform our three-ring circus but that did not deter us. It was so reckless and yet so carefree. Thankfully, there were no collisions. After some warm beverages we climbed back into our beetles and drove home safely. We could chalk up another adventure to our youthful existence.

But for the past few years, I have been facing the most daunting challenge of my life. Those lighthearted, free-wheeling days are long gone. Inside the hospital, my dear father was now lying motionless in bed, suffering from the late stages of ALS, better known as Lou Gehrig's disease. After three years of gradual physical decline at home, my father deteriorated from a strong vibrant seventy-year-old senior citizen to a weak and exhausted man. My mother was no longer able to care for him, and sadly, my father had to enter a care facility. The hard work of providing physical support for Dad eventually took its toll on my mother. It made her sick and weak and her doctor insisted that if Dad were not placed in a care facility, it would kill her. The only option with close proximity to their home was the local hospital where my siblings and I were born.

Prior to the diagnosis, his symptoms started with twitches in his arms which gradually progressed to other parts of his body. Initially, he was not overly concerned and considered it more of a nuisance related to aging, working too hard or a lack of some nutrient. As time passed however, the symptoms did not improve, and he noticed his muscles were getting weaker. The decline persisted and began to weigh on him emotionally. Until that point, my father was always a strong and healthy man and he could not fathom being sidelined by an illness. Gradually he noticed more tremor-like symptoms in his arms and legs, but it still did not deter him.

Dad cherished his social circle and loved hanging out with his buddies. They would take bicycle rides for exercise and fresh air. They would peddle for miles down farm laneways and country roads chatting and laughing away the time. Unfortunately, Dad would find himself getting more winded and tired than usual. It was then that my parents finally decided it was time to see their family doctor. This was a watershed moment for Dad. He did not believe in seeing a doctor about something he considered a minor problem. He would not allow himself to believe it was anything serious. He had assured himself that he was just getting old, and his muscles were understandably weakening. Regardless, he made the visit to his doctor.

In small country towns, medicine was not cutting edge. Country doctors were not faced with many obscure diseases. In the early days, they made house calls at ungodly times during the night. They dealt mostly with common illness, cuts, stitches, minor surgeries, and delivery of babies. His doctor advised him that it was likely aging that was affecting him. Mom and Dad convinced themselves that the doctor must be right and went about life as usual. Still, things were not getting any better. My parents found his twitches and tremors disturbing and they persisted in finding answers. They asked to be referred to a second doctor in town who was younger and had more advanced medical training and experience. This doctor ordered a series of tests to confirm his initial suspicions. The test was not for ALS. The diagnosis was the result of ruling out all other ailments through a comprehensive process of elimination. Diagnosing ALS was not a simple task. The results were not good, and the doctor's preliminary suspicions became a reality.

This doctor was very direct in his bedside manner and made it abundantly clear after his diagnosis that Dad was in the early stages of a terrible disease with no known cure. He prepared my mother with how this was going to drastically alter her life. Despite these warnings, little did any of us know how much life would change for all of us. This terrible disease did not progress in the usual fashion for my father. It impeded his ability to breathe at an early stage, which is typically in the final stages of ALS. There were times when, quite unexpectedly, he would black out and fall to the floor. My mother would struggle to lift him and revive him. She did not give up and devoted the next years of her life to his physical and emotional care.

There was nothing that my mother would not do for this man. The only thing that the rest of my family and I could do was spend as much time as possible with Dad and wait. Emotionally I wanted time and the progression of his illness to slow down. Logically I knew that was not going to happen. I was keenly aware as every day passed that I had one less day with my father on this earth. And most tragically, I knew that my father was cognizant of this too. His life was filled with days of waiting to die.

After my mother's call that fateful day in September 2001, I went back to work and the rest of my week was consumed with daily meetings, inspections, negotiations and charting the progress that we had made. I kept a keen eye on the aftermath of the attack on the World Trade Center.

For me, Friday is admiration day. It was the day when you could look back at the week's accomplishments. Burned out and needing a break, I had arranged to meet a few friends that night. We met up at a popular Italian restaurant,

Lina's, for beer, tapas, and conversation. My buddies Ron, Graham and Sanjay were old work mates that were in my circle of trust. I found it difficult to connect with anyone that I did not have much in common with, so most of my friends were work related. Besides being trustworthy and respectful to others, they could move from humorous to serious at a moment's notice. They were down to earth guys and loyal friends.

At least once or twice a month we found time to get together. When the weather permitted, we would meet for a round of golf. Our discussions often centered on political conflict that existed throughout the world. We could pivot from solving the world's problems to humoring ourselves with more comical events such as the best lies we ever told our mothers. In reality it was a mental health session enhanced by beer and food. It helped us maintain a level of sanity and helped us avoid expensive psychiatric bills as we navigated our way through a world of uncertainty, hypocrisy, and a good share of insanity.

This evening the topic was far more sobering. It centered on my impending trip to see my father. Although I did not believe there was anything to worry about, I was still apprehensive. My mother had called with this sort of cryptic message before and it had not amounted to anything consequential. We had grown accustomed to living with my father's illness. As we parted for the evening, they told me not to worry and to drive safely.

When I left the restaurant, I drove along the country roads to my modest home on the river. I lived alone as my first marriage had ended years ago and my girlfriend had her own house. All those construction projects miles from home were a challenge to family life. The naïve resort adventure that ended in disaster and near bankruptcy did not help. I had returned to my original career choice in construction but there was still frequent travel and absences involved. Now that I was on my own, it became imperative that I make time for my children. While on distant projects, I commuted endlessly by car or plane every other weekend so the kids and I could spend valuable time together. The four of us would take trips to parks, camp out, visit my parents and sometimes swing on ropes over a muddy stream for laughs. I even won a vacation trip allowing us some time in the Bahamas. One afternoon, I watched in horror as a sting ray circled my three kids while they played in the clear shallow ocean waters. Thankfully, the big fish was simply curious and it moved on. Throughout my work travels I maintained a home close to my children regardless of where the assignments took me. Fortunately, it all seemed to have worked out. My relationship with all three survived the challenges and now I am happy to have a close bond with them.

My late-night drive was nearing its end. The darkness of the night was broken by a brilliant crescent moon peeking through a spattering of layered clouds. A few minutes later, I was home and parking my beloved truck safely in the garage. I hoped to get some rest before the next day's long drive. Even though I was anxious I managed to get some sleep.

Saturday finally arrived. The orange sun was breaking over the horizon and a burst of light bounced off the river and illuminated the bedroom with a dazzling brilliance. I opened my eyes and gazed in awe at nature's wonder. The sun shimmered brightly through willow trees that looked like sentries lining the riverbank. I stood by the window to feel the warmth of the sun before showering and getting ready for my day. Afterwards I packed a small bag and did a final inspection before leaving the house. Outside, my chariot, a grey Ford F-150 crew cab short box awaited me. I loved driving my truck. Sitting high in traffic gave me a sense of security. After carefully backing it out of the narrow garage, I made my way to the backroads which would lead me to the highway that would eventually take me to my father. My sunglasses dimmed the piercing sunlight. Traffic was mild and I was eager to get on my way. It seemed like I would have perfect driving conditions.

It would take four hours of driving to get to my destination. I had my favorite road rock tunes playing and I settled in for the long trip home. Usually when I was on these long drives, my thoughts would be preoccupied with matters concerning myself. Today, my thoughts were centered on my mother's call and what the news could be. What could be so important? If dad had taken a turn for the worse, she would have told me. I kept telling myself that it was probably nothing consequential.

I took a mental journey back in time to the day two years past when my parents first summoned all of us to their home. My two sisters and my brother were already at my parents' house when I arrived. I could instantly feel that something was wrong when I walked through the door. The information they gave us decimated any shred of well-being and happiness that I had when I entered the house. They explained what they had been told by their doctor. We had no idea that my father had been experiencing symptoms and we could not imagine the mental anguish he must be feeling knowing his fate. They spoke to us in a devastatingly painful way, stopping every so often to wipe tears or to catch their breath. These were not the type of emotions that we were accustomed to seeing from our parents. This was unfamiliar territory. They were always certain and confident. They were our rocks. They were the ones that supported us emotionally. Everything changed in that moment. That day, ALS became front and center and oh so personal. It was that day that the four children became the parents, comforting, supporting, and caring for our mother and father. We now had to be their rocks.

My only previous awareness of ALS, which is an acronym for Amyotrophic Lateral Sclerosis, was the history pertaining to Lou Gehrig. We did not understand the disease and it left us bewildered and feeling helpless. ALS causes the death of neurons controlling voluntary muscles. It is a gradual disease which is generally painless and progresses to muscle weakness. It can result in abnormal fatigue of the arms and or legs, slurred speech, muscle cramps and twitches. There is no known cause but it is thought to be both environmental and genetic in nature. ALS leaves you about two to five years of life after being diagnosed. The remaining years are typically a life of severe disability.

My siblings and I were determined to find a solution and we were convinced that through research and tenacity we could restore my father's health. We were going to join forces, work through it and win this battle. The four of us delved into medical journals. My sisters spent many hours seeking advice from physicians and planning courses of action. We researched the disease and contacted organizations familiar with the care, progression, and treatments of ALS. The research was time consuming and it left us physically exhausted and emotionally drained. Unfortunately, we discovered that since it affected a relatively low number of people, medical research was extremely limited. There was no definitive cause and no known cure. Treatment primarily alleviated symptoms and did not attack the disease itself.

My father was assigned to Dr. Strong, who specialized

in ALS research and treatment. He was located at a university hospital about a two-hour drive away. I later learned
that this leading specialist was the younger brother of one
of my grade school buddies. Dad would have to visit Dr.
Strong every four to five months for updates and treatment.
Even with the medical supervision, Dr. Strong could offer
extraordinarily little in terms of stopping the progression
of the disease. Because it affected Dad's breathing at an
early stage, he would soon need the assistance of an
oxygen tank. He was given exercises to keep his muscles
active and try to slow the progression of this horrible
affliction.

The insidious nature of this disease is that although it
attacks the nervous system and renders the muscles useless
with the passing of time, the mind is unaffected. This leaves
the afflicted keenly aware of how it is altering their life and
impacting the lives of their loved ones. Being the strong
family leader that he always was, my father fought hard to
retain his dignity and keep up his spirits. In the early stages
of his diagnosis, he maintained his daily routine of
gardening and tending to his small backyard vineyard.
When he was no longer physically able, we would continue
to turn those purple grapes into a savory red wine for him.

In my younger years, Dad would make wine from grapes
he had purchased from California. He was so proud of his
winemaking and would talk endlessly about the finer art of
the craft. We would go to the local grower's warehouse and
buy cases of grapes that he ordered. Typically, he ordered
Zinfandel. Afterwards, we would drive the country roads
picking wild berries to blend in with the California grapes.
This gave the wine a deeper color and heavier flavor. During
wine season, we would crush the grapes, stomping them
with our feet and then giving them a final squeeze with an

old wine press that made its rounds between my uncles and my father.

The basement would be filled with the smell of the mash as it fermented. You would be covered with fruit flies if you approached those barrels during the fermentation process. Eventually, the mash would be sieved and juices would be transferred to demijohns for the final transformation into that fruit of the vine. Bottling time was fun as we filled and corked each new glass bottle and then laid them out in rows on racks to complete the aging process. As young children, my parents would allow us to taste the wine at dinner. Sometimes it would be vino mixed with 'gingerella.' They taught us to respect the drink at a young age.

Dad eventually planted his own vines in the backyard. When he was sick, we would help him harvest the home-grown grapes each year until finally his muscles could no longer support him. We also continued our search for a cure. He tried meditation and homeopathic treatments with no appreciable results. Each new method or attempt would fill my father with hope that would eventually be crushed as his condition continued to deteriorate. Over the next three years, we would watch as he gradually lost more control of his extremities and was confined to a wheelchair. It was a challenge for Dad to wheel himself around the house. The house was not built with wheelchair access in mind, and this contributed to many frustrating moments.

Prior to being confined to a wheelchair, my father was an avid ham radio operator and enjoyed contacting people around the world. To obtain his license, he had to learn Morse code and could only communicate using Morse code until he passed the voice operator exam. He would tell me how he could talk to people across the ocean when a phenomenon he called a skip would occur. He explained that happened when a signal would bounce off weather-related features and end up reaching other countries. After being confined to a wheelchair, he could no longer access his beloved radio in his specially equipped room in the basement.

When he was able bodied, Dad loved to tinker and taught himself to make things from bits and pieces of metal or wood. He assembled his entire radio station from parts he bought at the electronics shop and from other enthusiasts. He would make gadgets that we now take for granted. Once, after reading a magazine, he built a carbon arch welding machine and used it to build other bits of equipment and devices. Anything he built was solid and of good quality. If he felt something was of inferior construction, he would ask if it was made by a shoemaker. When I asked him what that meant, he would translate and ask if it was made half-assed.

His talents did not end there. Over the years he built an endless variety of homemade devices to use around the house. As his apprentice, I embraced the tradition and found myself following in his footsteps by using my hands and becoming a handyman myself. I attribute my skill with tools to my father. My household repairs would not be made were it not for his teachings.

My father was also a great negotiator. He refused to pay list price on big ticket items and on several occasions, I watched him in action. It proved to be my training ground for bartering as an adult. Everything I learned about reducing prices, I learned from my father. After I took up the practice, I found myself in a Woolworth's store with a friend of mine. We each needed a filing cabinet. The floor salesman was not willing to give us a discount for buying two cabinets. I asked for the manager and gave him my pitch.

He must have enjoyed the back and forth because we left with two filing cabinets for less than sticker price. On another occasion, I had my father with me as I tried to buy a stereo system at a reduced price. Regardless of how hard I tried to make a deal with the shop owner, he would not budge on the price and we walked away. After we left, my father told me he thought I may have pushed too hard. After that day, I refined my negotiating skills. I still love to haggle to get the best price. And every time I pay less than the list price, I think of my father. He would be proud of me.

Once he was confined to the wheelchair, Dad chose to limit his social contacts. At this point he was pretty much housebound with only my mother for companionship. It was impossible for him to even go outside. Four stairs led from the back door of the house to a concrete slab below. My brother and I decided to give Dad some freedom and built a raised wooden deck and ramp off the back door concealing those steps and covering the concrete slab. Dad could now get in and out of the house without assistance. We would no longer have to lift him up the stairs and in and out of the house. This gave him the freedom to go outdoors and escape into the world he loved. There he could breathe in the fresh air, and the scent of his ripening grapes and his beautiful flowers.

Many years ago, my father built a trellis above the back concrete patio. He planted vines around it which grew into a small vineyard producing sweet hanging red grapes. It was so cathartic to see Dad once again sit beneath his beloved grape vines and let the sun warm his face. We hoped the gentle breezes would take his mind off of his reality and the stresses and sadness that were a part of it. In those moments he must have been at peace with the world. It was bittersweet to watch him knowing that it would not last.

My mother, bless her heart, inherited the caregiver role. It consumed her every waking moment and most of her nights. Her life had become one of willing servitude. She was tireless and unrelenting in her duties. This was her husband and she did not take the vow, "in sickness and in health" lightly. We never heard her complain. Her caring defined her devotion and love for Dad. She would help him move about the house, clean his breathing equipment, order more tanks of oxygen, and still complete an endless list of daily household chores.

Eventually, my father lost all ability to take care of himself. He needed constant assistance and would struggle with simple tasks and yell out in frustration to get one of us to help him. Mom assisted him with anything and everything. She fed him and took care of the endless but necessary personal hygiene tasks he needed to live each day. I installed grab bars in the bathroom so he could help position himself. When his condition made it impossible for the two of them to share a bed, my mother bought him a new bed that could be adjusted with a hand-held control module. He slept in my old bedroom. She wanted him to be as comfortable as possible, but he still needed more care than she could handle alone. It became quite clear that Mom needed assistance. Outside help was eventually required during the night. She needed someone to relieve her for a few hours so she could get some sleep, regain her strength and deal with the next physically and emotionally draining day.

As fate would have it, this turned out to be a disaster. The assistant, who was referred by a local health care organization, would spend the night in the furnished family room and would tend to my father's needs during the night. Even with this help, Mom struggled to sleep. She felt uncomfortable having a stranger in the house at night, but it did provide her with some of the relief that she needed. Initially all seemed fine, but eventually her suspicions got the best of her. The assistant would arrive dressed somewhat inappropriately for her duties. One night mom heard commotion in the basement. When she went downstairs, she saw that the care giver had invited a friend over without permission. They had been socializing with little concern for my parents' comfort and need for sleep. My mother confronted the woman and an argument ensued. Mom ordered her to leave immediately.

It left my poor mother with a traumatic sense of distrust and she no longer wanted anyone in the house. This meant that she was once again fully responsible for Dad's care, which meant more sleepless nights for both her and my father. His breathing issues kept him awake during the night. He took many short naps rather than a long peaceful sleep. My father's physical needs were escalating to a breaking point for both of them.

The progression of the disease had been a roller coaster throughout his illness. Prior to my father's confinement in the wheelchair, I was fortunate to have been able to spend late summer weekends visiting with him. He could still walk at that time and we would spend hours in the yard shuffling through the grass, inspecting the fledgling grape vines that were creeping along the fence line and up the trellis. And every Sunday evening after a warm goodbye, I would get on the road for that long drive back to my home.

As time passed and the disease progressed, our family conversations became more subdued. The sadness we all felt as my father's condition continued to deteriorate left a pall on every call or visit. Even at my home and at my work-place, after a few sympathetic words from my friends, I would redirect the conversation. It was too hard to talk about it without making everyone feel bad. Regardless of how much heartfelt sympathy anyone conveyed to me, I was on a journey no one could possibly understand unless they had lived it themselves. My father's health eventually became a conversation everyone avoided. At the end of the day or evening, we would simply bid one another a good night. My friends would then give me a few words of support on the way out the door. There was really nothing else that anyone could do to help me. Besides my immediate family, I was alone on this journey.

One weekend after I completed the long drive home after visiting Dad, the phone started to buzz. It was my younger sister. She was frantic and spoke with trembling pain in her voice.

She sobbed, "Bob you need to come home right now!"

"What's wrong?"

She explained that Dad was in the hospital on life support. What was even more distressing for my family was that the doctor asked if we wanted to disconnect his life support system and end his life. He was on a life support system? End his life? I was in total shock.

"I was just there Paula and he was fine. What happened?"

She said he had suffered a breathing emergency and was rushed to the hospital where they put him on life support and administered oxygen. The news was unnerving and frightening. How could things have taken such a turn so quickly and so unexpectedly?

"I'm on my way," I told her.

Quickly, I grabbed some clean clothes and jumped back into the truck. By eleven p.m. I was on the road again returning to the place I had just left.

Once again, my thoughts were consumed with my father as I made the long drive to my parents' house. There was nothing unusual about this. My life since the diagnosis was centered on Dad and his deteriorating health. A man that I once thought was invincible was gradually losing control of his body and there was nothing any of us could do to change it. I continued to work, live my life, and raise my children, but in the quiet moments of the day every thought was with my father. I reflected on the long and painful journey from his initial diagnosis to the present. The countless drives back and forth between my parents' house and my home were typically filled with endless memories. My emotions would range from sadness to despair as I travelled the highway past the towns and open fields that would lead to my childhood home.

As I sped through the dark night passing one semi-truck after another, I could hear the deafening rumble of motorcycles approaching from behind. I thought to myself that they must have straight pipe mufflers. Since I was a motorcyclist, the sound was familiar but much louder than normal. In my rear-view mirror, I could see the bobbing headlights of approximately six bikes. The band of bikers caught up to me and the noise became deafening. The truck shook as I glanced over. I was well over the speed limit so I could only imagine how fast they were going. They seemed to accelerate and then sped past me. As they roared by, I noticed that familiar black leather vest with the skull and the three-patch emblem. I had just come within a few feet of a group of Hell's Angels making their way west. Miles up the road, I could still hear them even though they were far ahead of me.

Prior to this encounter my last meeting with the Hells Angels was at a Friday the Thirteenth Bike Festival when I accidently used their portable toilets. After a two-hour ride, I desperately needed to use the facilities. Everywhere I looked I saw lineups except at a bank of pristine toilets inside a cordoned off area. I thought I was lucky to be in the right place at the right time. The stars were aligning. Until I emerged from the toilet, I had no idea what I had just done. Several gang members were giving me threatening looks. As I lifted a leg over the roping my friend and riding partner Steve looked at me in total astonishment and said with a chuckle "If this gets ugly, you're on your own." Another lesson learned. Be aware of your surroundings or at the very least, learn to read the situation

I continued through the dark night driving down the highway finally reaching the country road that led to my hometown. The night was eerily dark and motionless as my solitary vehicle continued down the road flanked by open fields, ditches, and rows of telephone poles. I felt like I was alone in the world. As much as I tried, my anxiety did not allow me to observe speed limits that night. The trip took forty-five minutes less than usual. My thoughts were racing the entire drive and I prayed that I would get there before it was too late.

When I arrived at the hospital, I jumped out of the truck and ran to the entrance stopping at the nurse's station to ask what room my father was in. He was in intensive care. There I found my mother, sisters, and brother all sniffling and tightly holding one another. My father's dimly lit room was engulfed in grief where he lay unconscious but still alive. His breathing machine was pulsating as the monitor was beeping out his heartbeat. A priest was close by holding his bible and softly reciting prayers.

We recounted the evening's events in disbelief and wondered what the next steps would be. We told ourselves that it was not Dad's time yet. We were not ready to lose him. The entire family sat in the room until dawn anticipating death and at the same time fearing it. We wanted to be with my father as he took his last breath. He had always been there for us. As daybreak lit up the room, relatives started arriving. My mother insisted that we contact his specialist at the university to get his opinion. After a couple of long and wrenching hours of waiting, the doctor authorized Dad's transfer to the university hospital.

Once they wheeled him into the ambulance, we rushed to our vehicles and made our way to the hospital. That two-hour drive took forever. Upon arrival, he was immediately taken to the intensive care unit. We wanted to be close to him, but we could only see him from a distance. He was placed on a bed as doctors and nurses connected tubes and sensors to his body. They worked with speed and precision. The room was lit up and fully equipped with instruments, readouts, and machines. A breathing mask was placed on his face as he lay there, and we anxiously waited for something to happen.

To our astonishment and sheer joy, within an hour he was wide awake, alert and propped up in his ICU bed. We thought it was a miracle. Science and a well-trained medical staff proved to be the true heroes. Later, the doctor arrived and explained that oxygen was not in his best interest after he collapsed. In fact, what he needed was more carbon dioxide. It was an honest mistake that would not have been understood by someone who does not specialize in this disease. We were overcome with emotion, relieved and so happy to see Dad awake and alert. This was a nerve shatteringly close call. We hugged one another and praised Mom for her stubborn refusal to disconnect my father's life support. My strong, loving Italian mother once again pulled us back from the brink.

After a couple of hours had passed, I was able to speak to his nurse. She told me how she was enamored by my father's character and personality. She felt a connection to him and found it pleasing and comforting to be near him and speak with him. That kind nurse became our source of information and kept us well informed of all developments throughout his stay in the hospital. It was easy to understand what she meant. My father was a very handsome, dark complexioned man with defined features. He could have been James Garner's stand in. He was strong and at the same time warm and gentle. He loved to laugh and made friends with ease. He was a principled, hardworking, and respectful man who loved life, his family, and his friends. He reflected his upbringing.

He was the second oldest of a family of ten children born in a small village south of Rome in the province of Frosinone Italy. They lived on a rural farm working tirelessly day in and day out tending to their crops and farm animals, scratching out a meager existence. All the farm buildings that he called home were made of hand laid limestone and wooden roofs. Eventually, this hard life of toil convinced the family that somehow someone needed to travel to America, work hard and send money back home. As the oldest male, it fell on his shoulders to make the journey to the land of opportunity.

My father was sponsored by a distant relative who had already become naturalized years earlier. Dad arrived in North America in 1952 when he was only twenty-four years old. He crossed the ocean aboard a ship with other immigrants and soldiers coming to start a new life after the devastation of World War II. The rest of the family remained in

Italy to carry on. Over the years, he in turn sponsored seven of his siblings to join him. Together, they raised families within ten miles of each other. They all got their start by working on farms or taking jobs at the local factory. As the years passed, life became surprisingly good as they worked hard and raised their families.

And now it seemed unfathomable that this man who had endured such hardship, had survived a war and who had the courage to start a new life in a country foreign to him, would have his life ended by an invisible enemy that no one fully understood. He had managed to overcome every other obstacle and adversity that had come his way. We just could not believe that he would not be able to overcome this disease. My father had always seemed invincible and yet day after day, week after week we were watching his body deteriorate. How could this be happening?

During our wait at the hospital, I got to know my dad's specialist. Dr. Strong offered me his personal phone number in case I needed to reach him with any questions or concerns. I was honored that he trusted me with his number. It was obvious that the doctor was old beyond his years. The responsibility and stresses of his work as a specialist trying to find suitable treatment for his dying patients had left a toll on him. Even though this likeable man possessed a positive attitude, I could only imagine by his completely gray hair and his haggard facial features that he had seen too much grief during his career. Most doctors get to work miracles and save gravely ill patients. Dr. Strong went to work every day knowing that he was unable to save anyone under his care from their inevitable demise. He had to be keenly aware that the day may never come when he could.

After my father was revived, the doctor asked me to talk to him and try to convince him that his quality of life would improve with a tracheotomy and a breathing tube. He explained that in his condition it would help with his breathing and the episode we just experienced could be avoided in the future. While unsure of his reaction, I approached my father with the recommendation. He was dead set against it. I suspect his reaction was prompted by his fear that things were not going to improve by taking this drastic step. He still believed that a treatment would materialize soon and cure this terrible disease. He was a very hopeful, positive thinking man and I did not want to take away the one thing that he seemed to have an abundance of.

Sensing that my father needed some encouragement, the doctor introduced me to a pleasant lady in her sixties sitting in her wheelchair with a tracheotomy tube. This delightful lady emphatically reassured me that it was best to have the tracheotomy. She told me it made her life so much easier. I asked if she would sit with my father and help him with this decision. She was happy to help, which in turn took so much pressure off of me. My father was a softy when it came to women. Having five sisters probably taught him a bit about chivalry.

I wheeled the lady to my father's bedside in ICU and introduced them to one another. They hit it off almost immediately, chattering away about their lives and recent developments. Finally, the topic of the surgery came up and she was masterful in convincing him that he too, should have it done. I am sure that her charm played a significant role in my father's decision to consent to the procedure. As promised, the minor surgery did help him breathe better and seemed to take a burden off of him. He no longer had to fear the simple act of breathing anymore. It took some getting used to, but he eventually came to accept it as part of his life.

After getting over all these hurdles, the family felt the need to release and celebrate the recent win of bringing dad back to life. We gathered at a local restaurant for lunch, hugged one another and raised a glass to better days ahead. Our eyes were filled with tears, our conversation was filled with joyous relief and our hearts were filled with love for my father. It was not his time yet. We had more days to look forward to, with him gracing our lives.

During that ordeal, Dad spent several weeks at the university hospital. Mom was housed at a local Church dormitory during his stay. Afterwards, he returned home, and they did their best to cope with their new way of life. He was now connected to a machine. Both my mother and father had to live with the new conditions and find ways to deal with the constant challenges they faced.

Months after my father left the university hospital, I called Dr. Strong. I knew he had to be busy, but he still took my call. Dad was home again, and the trauma of his potentially imminent demise had passed. No longer physically active, my father spent most of his time watching television. He happened to see a medical program relating to ALS and how a new drug showed signs of positive clinical results. Dad called me right after that program ended and asked me to call the doctor at the university and see if he could prescribe the drug to him.

At this point I would have done anything to help my father. Even though I was apprehensive and had lost so much hope by this time, the call was made. I never wanted to let my father down and I was concerned that the momentary hope he had would turn to disappointment once again. To have access to this drug seemed improbable since it was experimental and was only being used in clinical trials at this point. The doctor was gracious and accommodating with his time. He confirmed that it was indeed an experimental drug and it only showed limited promise to patients in the early stages of ALS. It was disheartening to hear. Now I had to pass this information on to my father who I knew would be deeply disappointed. I wanted to give him hope, but my father's disease had progressed well beyond the stage where the drug could have any positive impact.

It was only when they could no longer cope at home, that they admitted Dad to the local hospital. This final relocation would evolve into a whole year in a hospital bed. Mom once again approached each day with tireless devotion and conviction. She would eat a quick breakfast and would then make the ten-minute drive to be with her beloved husband, looking after his every need. Mom was in her early sixties now, but she did not get her driver's license until she was well into her fifties. Being a relatively inexperienced driver, she was only comfortable driving into town and back home again. At the hospital, she would feed him, bathe him, read to him, and make him comfortable by changing his sheets and positioning him in his bed. They would fondly speak to one another, sharing cheerful stories of their youth and life back in Italy.

At times, Dad would have his moments of anger and frustration. He had a hard time accepting his fate. Not being able to perform the simplest of tasks would irritate him. It broke our hearts knowing that there was little if anything we could do to alleviate his suffering. While he slept, Mom would try to do the same sitting next to his bed. At eight p.m. she would return home, eat some dinner, and then go to bed without her beloved husband by her side. This was her daily routine throughout his stay at the hospital. My mother and father became well known to the staff. The nurses appreciated all the help that Mom provided by doing many of the duties that they would have had to do. They all became like family to them. The staff would stop in and greet Mom and Dad each morning providing a needed break from the endless hours of silent waiting. Dad's brothers and sisters would provide needed social when they visited. They were waiting and hoping for something that would never come. Their dream was freedom from this horrible disease that had turned all our lives upside down and robbed them of a future. We envisioned freedom as recovery from this disease. Little did we know that my father did not see it the same way.

Summoned home once again, I made the long drive to my little town as I had done so many times before. My mind was filled with questions and my heart was filled with despair. What awaited me? Whatever the new development was, I knew it could not be good.

9

DAD'S STORY

The trip to visit Dad seemed short and time passed quickly as endless thoughts churned in my head. Before I knew it, I was approaching my familiar hometown and the hospital where I was born. Because of his physical needs, this was the place where Dad was now forced to live. In reality, this was not home, and this was not living. It was a mere existence. He was trapped in a lifeless body and living in a world that in no way resembled his former life. He yearned to be at home in the place he felt connected to, the place he built and the place where he raised his family. And sadly, that was something we could not make happen.

I parked the truck and made my way to the brick building. After I greeted the hospital staff, I walked past them with purpose. My visits were like missions. It was something I wanted to do and yet dreaded at the same time. I was accustomed to visiting him every two or three weeks and we would just sit and talk about everything and anything he chose. It was reassuring to see the man that had raised me, and at the same time, it was devastating to see him trapped in a shell of a body.

Today, however, I was there by request. Something was different and I was unsettled as I entered his room. I greeted him with my customary hug and kiss on his forehead as he lay next to the open window. A cool breeze was drifting into the room and sunlight splashed the wall. From his window he had a view of the VW dealership and the farmland beyond. His room was pale blue with all the typical medical connections on the wall. There was a bathroom in the corner and a few pictures hanging on the walls depicting pastures and landscape. He had a private room which made life much easier for him and my mother. I reached for a visitor's chair nearby and pulled it closer to my father's bedside. Now that the disease had taken a firm hold of his nervous system, he was unable to move and could only slightly adjust his neck and shift his eyes. His tracheostomy tube was connected, and I could hear his breaths as the ventilation machine pulsated. I reached for his bed control module and slowly adjusted his back thirty degrees upwards so that he could sit up and we could see each other.

These visits left me with a feeling of profound sadness that I had never felt before in my life. I wanted to be strong for both of us and I did my best to shield him from my despair. In my mind, I struggled with how this disease had ravaged the vital, energetic person I had looked up to as a hero my entire life. He was the person I tried to model my life after. Withering away in the bed beside me was an honest, respectable, and decent man. Why him? He lived a moral life, raised a good family and was always there for anyone that needed him. He did not deserve this. He looked at me with the eyes of someone who felt defeated. I responded with a forced smile. We sat for a moment in silence.

"How are you feeling today Dad?" I did not expect a

response. It was a feeble attempt to make conversation, but it was the best I could do. Appearing upbeat and positive was difficult when all I wanted to do was curl up in a ball and cry. I was not that good of an actor and it always concerned me that he could tell that my positive attitude was forced and fake.

He looked at me, paused and then said, "I want you to know that I have been thinking long and hard and I have decided that my time has come. Next Saturday these machines will be shut off."

Without expressing any emotion, he continued, giving the final instructions to me that he and Mom had decided on. The final assault in his battle with the disease was about to come to an end and the disease won. He had reached his breaking point and he felt he could no longer keep up the fruitless fight to continue his life. He wanted to pass away and end this losing struggle for survival that had consumed him and Mom these last few years. He had come to the realization that living meant more than merely existing.

"Bobby, this is no life to live. I spend my days lying in a hospital bed with only memories to relive and wait for death to come and take me away. Look at your poor mother. She is stressed and weak from taking care of me. She has been with me every day now and I can see her getting weaker and more tired. I can't do that to her anymore." He was resolute.

As I looked at him, tears started to well up in my eyes. I knew he was right, but I was not ready to let go of my father. Dad put on a brave front, but I knew he must be frightened. Although he seemed ready to let go physically, I knew that he would never want to leave his family if there was a better alternative. I studied his face and could not help but notice a sense of relief in his demeanor and facial expression. I believe that Dad had come to terms with his mortality. He told me that he hated to go and leave Mom alone. He was sad to leave his children and grandchildren, and he wanted to know that we would be alright without him. I reassured him that we were all doing well with good jobs and healthy families and that his job was now to take care of himself and not worry about us. He had hoped to see the grandkids get married and have children of their own one day. I assured him that he did a great job raising us and that we were all well prepared for whatever life had in store for us. I wanted him to know that he could be proud and comforted to know that his job was complete on earth. He told me he had already advised his doctor and the hospital staff of his decision. There was a DNR - Do Not Resuscitate notice over his bed.

We spoke about life after death and how we envisioned it. My father's faith had been shaken by the last few catastrophic years. He rolled his eyes and questioned the existence of God and why would He let this happen to him? We could not find any answers. I assured him that life would be much better on the other side and that we would all be together again one day. I tried my best to reassure him, but he was not totally convinced. Little did I know that one day I would also be questioning my faith just like my father was doing.

He was not angry or agitated. I suspect he was in a state of acceptance and happy that he would be relieved of this endless suffering. I was at peace knowing that he was comfortable with his final wishes. As much as I loved my father and wanted him to stay with us, I knew that he was correct to end his ordeal. He felt it was better to leave on his own terms rather than continue to suffer indefinitely knowing his condition would only continue to deteriorate. I knew he did not come to this decision easily and I had to respect his choice.

After much discussion, he provided some final instructions, "I need you to watch out for your mother after I'm gone. Check in with her every week. I need to know that you will follow through."

I emphatically assured him. "You can count on me Dad. We will all be there for her and keep her safe and secure. I'll check in every week."

He continued, "Don't let her get remarried to someone who will rob her of her money."

"Don't worry Dad," I replied with a bit of a smile.

To his very last days my father remained a practical man. My parents were the epitome of frugal. My dad liked to say he never passed a penny on the ground that he did not pick up, or that he was so tight he squeaked. My mother would constantly remind me to save my money. She would tell me to become a lawyer or doctor because they make a good living. For two people who worked at unskilled laborer jobs they managed to send money back to Italy, raise a family, build a house, own a car and be free of debt. They knew what they were talking about when it came to finances. Hard living during difficult times taught them some valuable life lessons. Even under these trying circumstances, my father still felt a responsibility to pass on his knowledge. He even made sure that we knew how to decant wine from a demi john before he passed away. However, it was unfortunate that my father never had a life insurance policy. He felt it was a waste of money. Regardless, he left my mother with a comfortable life, saved funds and his pension.

With his resolve to close the chapter on his suffering, I wanted to sit and talk about his life and about the life we all shared with him. I wanted to know more about where he grew up and what he experienced as a young man. I had heard some of his stories over the years but now it seemed important to hear them once again. Even in his weakened state he obliged, and I sat listening as he reminisced about events that he experienced and some that we experienced together. Although I was eager to hear his stories of days gone by, most importantly I just wanted to hear his voice. The thought of never hearing him speak again was unbearable.

He started by talking about our life in that small house surrounded by farmland on Martin Drive. We talked about our annual vacations to places like Niagara Falls or The Lady of Fatima shrine in Ohio. When visiting Niagara Falls, we always stayed at the same motel across the street from the Kellogg's cereal factory where you could smell corn-flakes baking in the air. We were far from the tourist attractions of Niagara Falls but we did not care. It was exciting to be away from home sleeping somewhere other than in our own beds and eating food that my mother had not prepared. As much as I loved my mother's cooking, it was far more exciting to eat a hotdog and French fries smothered in ketchup. That type of food was a novelty that was not served at home.

We reminisced about how we would stop every hour or so at roadside rest-stops to picnic or to open the hood of the old '49 to cool the engine and release steaming coolant. Back then, cars were not as reliable as they are now. Driving on the highways in those days was not about speed. It was more about getting there. For Dad, it was about stopping along the way to stretch, have a picnic and take a rest with his family. The journey was always as much a part of the trip as the destination. We usually travelled in caravans of two or three cars loaded with kids, food, hibachis, and toys. If you broke down on the highway in those days, truckers were there to help. They were highly respected, and they always stopped to assist a stranded motorist. It was not unusual to see a big rig stopped behind a broken-down vehicle and see the trucker help to change a tire or check under the hood.

Years later my brother became a long hauler himself. I always thought that those road trips may have inspired him. He tells me that the days of help on the road from truck drivers is long past. Economics have turned trucking into a dog-eat-dog business. Today the roads are full of trucks delivering everything we surround ourselves with. I have not seen a trucker helping a stranded motorist in a long while. Of course, better built cars and cell phones have made road-side problems easier to address.

The Ohio trips always started early in the morning and ended before dusk. The longest trip that we ever made was the drive to Providence, Rhode Island to visit my father's cousin Guido who had left the priesthood to live a less secular life. This was to be the one and only time we visited him. The drive passed quickly because I slept most of the way. When my siblings and I were not sleeping, the four of us passed the time by belittling and annoying one another in the back seat. My mother would periodically turn around and threaten to leave us on the side of the road. If that did not work, she would turn around and tell us we would be sorry for not listening to her as she took a swipe at us. She rarely made contact. Retrospectively, I think she had no intention of hitting us. I think she just wanted us to believe that she would. I am guessing that they prayed for the moments when we would exhaust ourselves and fall asleep.

The highlight of the trip was a visit to an amusement

park in Providence. I recall being on a circling scrambler like ride with my sister Hilda. As the ride moved faster and went higher, I could feel my little sister slowly slipping out of the ride. Panicked, I held her tight and yelled at the operator to stop. To my stark terror, he seemed to speed up the ride. He apparently misunderstood our screams to stop. Relief does not describe what I felt when it finally slowed down and we were able to disembark the terrifying ride. As always, it was all caught on my father's movie camera. Viewing that footage years later, I realized it was not nearly as dramatic as I recalled.

It was during this visit to Rhode Island that my mother exposed a side of herself that I did not know existed. While shopping at a department store, I caught her switching price tags on articles of clothing. Price tags were easily switched before the advent of pre-perforated stickers. She did it with the confidence and skilled precision of someone who had mastered the art. As a young child I was horrified to see the person who had taught me right from wrong, do something that seemed dishonest. Growing up in a devout Catholic family, I was very much aware of the ten commandments, particularly the one regarding stealing. I was shocked to know that my loving, God fearing mother had a criminal streak. Could there be circumstances where it was alright to defy God's teachings? As confused as I was, I did not dare ask for clarification.

My father was a big camera and movie buff and owned an assortment of vintage and modern equipment. He was always fully loaded for any and every occasion that arose with a camera for snapshots and an eight-millimeter for home movies. Whether it was a rite of passage, a family occasion or just the kids playing in the backyard, he loved to take pictures and make movies. After the movies were developed, we could not wait to see ourselves on celluloid. He even dabbled in special effects with such absurdities as five kids magically jumping out of a barrel one at a time. Our young lives were well documented on my father's films. At times it seemed like a nuisance to stop and pose for a picture when we just wanted to get on with whatever it was that we were doing, but now I am grateful for the time that he invested in memorializing our lives and preserving our memories.

Astronomy was another of my father's passions. He was fascinated by the heavens. This interest prompted him to buy a telescope and rig his camera equipment up to it so he could take photos of the Moon, Mars, Saturn, Jupiter, and Mercury. It captured my imagination as well and became a common interest that bonded us. I was amazed when I first laid eyes on a magnified image of Saturn with its rings and moons. My father and I would spend nights together gazing at celestial objects. My life was so entwined with his and his death was going to leave an unimaginable void. I could not envision my life without my father.

Now our discussion turned to when my father built our new house and the winter nights when we would drive six miles through storms to check on the water pump in the partially built home. Driving through the cold and dark on the snow-covered roads, we seemed be the only vehicle with somewhere to go. Visibility was sometimes near zero. My dad always insisted that we had to go to ensure the basement did not flood and then freeze. For me, these trips were exciting adventures as we blazed through what I perceived to be a blizzard in the '59 Plymouth. When you are a young kid, things quite often seem more dramatic than they are while being oblivious to actual potential threats. In my mind the drive through a routine snowstorm was an adventure. I was totally unconcerned with the actual problem and oblivious to my father's real fear that the culmination of his hard work and sacrifice to provide us with a better life could be destroyed by the inclement weather.

I reminded him that he would tell me I was his best hunting dog. When we would hunt pheasant, quail, or rabbit, it was my job to flush it out while he took aim and shot it out of the sky as I ran for cover. He was a surprisingly good shot. In hindsight, I realize it was not good practice to have your child find the wild game. However, chasing pheasants through the corn fields was big fun for a young kid. The pheasant would run through the rows of corn rather than fly away. I would find myself chasing the birds until they finally took flight, and my father would shoot and bring them back down to earth. He owned a double barrel twelve-gauge savage shotgun that he eventually handed down to my brother. I never liked eating wild meat, but I loved hunting with my dad. His motto was you eat what you kill. He was never one to waste.

We once again reverted to stories about life on Martin Drive. Once when I was not yet a teenager, I begged for a BB gun for Christmas. Neither of my parents approved and tried to steer me to other options. However, one morning a few days before Christmas there was a suspicious looking neatly wrapped present with my name on it under the tree. The gift looked like it was about the right size to contain a BB gun. While my parents were away on a shopping trip, I carefully peeled the tape off one end. As I folded back the paper my eyes and mouth opened wide in total amazement when I read that it contained a BB gun. Carefully I slipped the box out of the wrapping and opened it with shear excitement. Inside was a lever action BB gun. After loading it, I took it outside and waited for a bird to come within range. Taking aim, I fired and hit a sparrow singing in the tree. The bird fell to the ground and fluttered until it stopped moving. It did not feel good to see the creature struggle. I felt a horrible sadness as I watched it slowly go limp and die. That bird was the first and last animal I ever shot. I returned the gun to its wrapper and used my best acting skills when it was time to open the present. After my experience with the bird, I only used the gun for target practice. My father found it useful to scare birds off his grape vines. I treasured the gun and I still have it today.

One of the most foolish, terribly naïve, and dangerous games we ever played was to get decked out as cowboys and rustlers. The neighborhood kids met up and chose sides. Then using real pellet and BB guns we hid behind the trees and barrels. The shooting started and did not end until one of the rustlers got a pellet lodged in his hand. That experience taught us the danger of any type of gun if it is not used properly. After that day, we stopped playing that game with live rounds and cap guns became our new weapon of choice.

I now had a burning question for Dad. It was something that puzzled me for many years, but I never had the nerve to ask for clarification. It was regarding an incident that happened while I was still a teenager living at home.

"Dad," I said, "do you remember that time I lost my wallet?"

My question brought a smile to his face as his eyes widened. He knew exactly what I was talking about. It was nice to see him smile even if only for a moment. That did not happen too often anymore. The wallet incident occurred when I was an older teenager and like many boys that age, we held this common belief that having a condom in your wallet was a sacred rite of passage. This proved to be more for show than necessity as the occasion to use one never arose, at least not for me. I did not seem to have the gift of sweeping a girl off her feet and out of her clothes. Since it sat in my wallet for an extended period, it probably was well passed its expiration date. This did not matter because it was mostly a boy's bragging tool. It was not easy to acquire one and we made sure that all our friends knew what was in our wallets.

The day I lost my wallet started out like any other Saturday during the summer. My friend and I were hanging out at the beach in the National Park at the edge of town. After a few hours of soaking up some sun with the transistor radio blaring out tunes and listening to the surf we packed up and walked back to the car. We then headed to the A&W to grab some Papa burgers and fries for lunch. A&W was the last of the dying breed of drive-in restaurants. It was the only place in town where you could relax in your car, order a meal, and then have it delivered on a tray that got clipped to your lowered car window. Once our order arrived, I reached in my back pant pocket for my wallet, only to realize my wallet was not there. I then searched each of my other pockets hoping it would somehow miraculously be found.

Panic, fear, and anxiety took a hold of me. I must have lost my wallet at the beach. My friend paid the bill. We wolfed down our meals and anxiously waved a hostess over to take our tray. We then raced back to the beach and combed the entire area and parking lot. Thinking someone may have found it and turned it in, we went to the administration office and asked if anyone had found a wallet. No luck was to be had. I was panicked thinking about having to replace all my documents. Consumed with worry, it occupied my every thought for a couple of days.

I could not tell my parents. They would think I was irre-
sponsible.

A few days later, while I was at work driving a forklift
loading trucks with produce, I saw my dad on the warehouse
dock heading in my direction. This was extremely unusual.
Why was he here? I shifted into forward gear and drove
towards him and stopped.

"Hey Dad, what's up?" I asked.

He looked at me and then reached into his back pocket
and produced my wallet.

My father asked, "Did you lose something Bobby?"

I was shocked. "Thanks Dad. Where did you find it?"

He said, "A friend of mine from work found it at the
park and knew you were my son."

I took it from him and was ready to slip it into my pocket
when he said, "Have a look inside and make sure nothing is
missing."

With a sense of bewilderment, I opened the wallet and
carefully checked each compartment. My driver's license
and all my other cards were there. Even the five-dollar bill
was still in the bill compartment. When I got to the slot that
held the condom, I noticed that it was gone. It was the only
thing that was missing.

My father asked, "Well? Is everything there?"

Embarrassed and not sure how to handle the situation, I
responded, "Yup, it's all there."

He looked at me with fake concern.

"Everything is good Dad. Thanks."

"Ok. See you at home," he responded as he walked
away.

I knew something was up. Who took the condom? Was it
my dad's friend trying to save me from embarrassment or
was it my father? It did not take a rocket scientist to figure it

out. I knew it was my father but there was no way that I could bring up the subject without admitting that I carried a condom in my pocket. I figured it was his way of saying without saying anything that he knew. All these years later he confirmed that it was indeed him that removed the condom from my wallet. We now shared a good laugh. It was funny how through all those years we held this common secret and neither of us said a word to the other.

My father now turned his attention to some of the sad and horrific tragedies the family endured while living in America. Dad's brother, Uncle Pat (Pasquale) had two sons, Michael, and David. Michael loved to fish and would spend hours at the local dock calmly waiting for that prize catch to come along. The concrete dock and warehouses protruded into the lake and had several ramps where boats with low gunnels could be unloaded. These ramps were sometimes subjected to high water levels and crashing waves. And like many boat ramps, they were slippery with moss. Michael, who was married with two children, made a fateful error by walking down one of these slippery ramps. He fell into the water where he drowned. Several years later, his brother David died tragically in a mobile trailer fire after making himself a late-night meal and falling asleep. These events shook the family and turned my Uncle Pat and his wife Aunt Joan into new parents once again.

The day seemed to be passing far too quickly and I was eager to hear more about his life as a young man back in Italy. Now that time was precious and his days were numbered, I wanted to know more about his life before the opportunity would be forever taken from me. I knew from previous discussions that he survived World War II as a young teen. It became clear to me as he shared his story that my youthful adventures, as exciting as I may have thought they were, paled in comparison to his.

His life started on a small farm in a countryside village named Ceprano with a population of several thousand. It was located just over sixty miles south of Rome near the Liri River. Ceprano was part of the Papal States from the sixth century and became part of the Republic of Italy in 1946. It was in the Lazio region which dates to 328 BC. It still holds some ruins in Arce dating back to the Roman Empire.

My father was born on the farm during the summer of 1928 on the third of August. There were no hospitals nearby and childbirth was via midwives. The Catholic Religion was very much engrained in the Italian culture thanks in no small part to The Emperor Constantine who declared Christianity as the official doctrine back in the early 300s BCE. My father, Giovanni Battista, was named after John the Baptist. Many Italian names are derived from Catholic Saints. In the year of Giovanni's birth, Benito Mussolini became Prime Minister after the death of Giovanni Giolitti, one of Italy's most popular Prime Ministers. The following year The Vatican became an independent state under The Lateran Pacts negotiated by Mussolini. Ambrogio Damiano Achille Ratti was the first sovereign of The Vatican as Pope Pius XI.

Dad's mother Nonna Maria and his father Nonno Giuseppe were poor farmers leading a simple country life. My grandfather's family dates back to ancient Hebrew origins followed by a migration to Italy and Catholicism. The farm was a primitive collection of buildings handed down through the family. It was surrounded by tall trees and brush with narrow trails leading to the main roads and other farms. The roads were merely dirt and gravel with a row of weeds in the middle of the laneway. For transportation, there were only bicycles unless you were lucky enough to own a scooter. The only cars in the village were owned by doctors and the local taxi company.

In the late 1960s when I was thirteen years old, my mother, my baby sister and I travelled to her ancestral home. This would be the first time since 1954 that my mother would return to Italy. We traveled aboard a four engine DC-8 jetliner to Rome. The plan was that my mother and my sister would stay at her parents' home in nearby San Giovanni, and I would spend my time in Italy at my father's childhood farm in Ceprano.

Once there I experienced Italian road rage for the first time when we left the airport and travelled through the narrow streets of Rome. It was an angry exchange between several drivers all trying to squeeze through the same narrow street at the same time. Horns were blaring, hands were flailing, and people were yelling at one another in angry high pitched Italian voices. At least fifteen minutes were spent watching men get out of their vehicles and with the assistance of hand jesters, scream at one another. The only people making any progress through that mess were the scooters that dodged and weaved through the jammed traffic with their buzzing two cycle motors. The fashionably dressed girls riding side saddle on the back seat of the scooters captured my imagination. After each of the protesters had an opportunity to express their angry point of view, they got back into their vehicles and tried to slowly escape the traffic standstill.

I quickly learned during my visit, that this type of spontaneous event was common and would explode randomly in the narrow streets as high-strung drivers hurried to their destinations. My father always said that being Italian meant that we cannot speak with our hands tied behind our backs.

It was in that moment that I fully understood what he meant. It was here that I realized my family was not an aberration and that hand gestures are an integral part of the Italian language. It was also here that I realized that talking with our hands was genetic and transcontinental.

After the traffic started to clear, we slowly wove our way through the street. Driving out of Rome we passed the iconic Coliseum and the Roman ruins before escaping to the lush tranquility of the green countryside. After an hour-long drive, we finally reached my mother's sleepy village in San Giovanni. There we met her family. After the obligatory hugging, double cheek kissing, glass of wine and high-pitched operatic chatter, we took a twenty-minute ride to my father's farm. Here I met his side of the family only to repeat the whole greeting process all over again. They spoke with loud voices throwing their arms into the air in sheer excitement as we approached. Quickly chairs were set out. Bottles of wine and an assortment of cheeses, olives and bread appeared. I looked around at the farm's grey stone structures which surrounded a small dirt courtyard. It was there that feasts would be held at the end of the working day, at the large handmade grand wooden table.

One of the buildings housed my grandparents' bedroom with an adjoining kitchen. Another two-story structure had a cow barn downstairs and a bedroom upstairs. It seemed to me that this was something that you would see in the 11th century in Italy. A third building held more bedrooms that once housed ten kids and a gathering room. There was no running water and the kitchen and each bedroom had only one electrical outlet. It seemed primitive even in the nine-teen-sixties. The bathroom was nothing more than a reed hut secluded from the buildings. There was a hole in the bench seat and little lizards would poke their heads in and out to watch you do your business. I recall trying to catch one only to be left with a piece of his tail between my fingers. Naively, I placed it in my wallet believing that the lizard would grow back. At night, it was downright creepy if you needed to make a quick run to the bathroom.

To get water, I learned that we had to harness the large grunting ox to the wooden cart and go to the well down the dirt road and fill a forty-five-gallon drum. Since the farm did not have running water, this would be used for baths, drinking water and cooking. It would take an hour to fill the containers by lowering and raising the wooden bucket into the community well. Back at the farm, the men joined forces to lower the barrel of water from the cart.

The orchards and crops were down the road where figs, grapes, tomatoes, cucumbers, corn, rye, and wheat were grown. As a kid from the other side of the ocean, I was not accustomed to the eating habits of my ancestors. For breakfast I insisted on Corn Flakes. This meant we had to go to town where the local kids would laugh at my footwear. There, in one of the small general stores we were able to purchase Corn Flakes. I could not bring myself to drink the white stuff I watched my grandfather squirt out of his cows. I eventually adapted to drinking cow milk mixed with coffee after I realized it gave it a better flavor.

I would watch my Nonna make ricotta cheese from goat milk. She would put the milk in a large pan and let it solidify into cheese under the sun. I am sure there was more to it, but that was the only part I saw and in my young mind that was all there was to it. Once I visited my father's childhood farm, it was easier to visualize and understand the environment he grew up in. Recently I was able to visit the old farm once again. What remained were remnants of what it had once been. Today the property is uninhabited. While the

land is still owned by the family, it was left to the forces of
nature and decay after my grandparents passed away. It is a
stark reminder of how life was during my father's time in
Italy.

In his youth, my father spent most of his time helping on
the farm. His daily duties included milking the cows,
fetching eggs from the chicken coop, and hoeing and
harvesting the fields. Being the oldest male child in the
family, his duties took on more responsibility as he grew
older. He would harness the ox and plow the fields. Most of
my father's life in the 1930s and 1940s centered around the
day-to-day routine of waking at dawn, heading to the fields
with his father and his siblings and working all day till sun
down with a few breaks. The men wore fedoras, long baggy
pants and white shirts while the women were dressed in long
flowing dresses with red scarves. Lunch would be delivered
to the fields by his sisters. The site of baskets covered with
checkered tablecloths was the announcement of break time.
Under a shade tree they would relax, laugh, share cheese,
olives, homemade wine, capicola and bread before returning
to the hard back-breaking work of tending to the fields. All
their food and wine were hand crafted on the farm. The
vineyard was revered and well-tended to. The workday
ended at dusk and they would feast until it was time for bed.
The next day would always be a repeat of the previous day.

Other than feasting and socializing with other family
members, there were not many options for entertainment
after work. As far as they were concerned, this was how
everyone lived. They did not dream of a different way of life
because they had never experienced an existence outside of
their sprawling country farm. This was all my father knew,
all his parents knew, and all their ancestors had ever known.
They had heard stories about Rome, and Naples' beaches

where the lifestyle was much more cosmopolitan, but they
never considered leaving the security of their farm. Besides
leaving their family, what held them back was money which
was a scarce commodity. To leave was an improbable
dream.

They thought stories of life in Rome were likely
overblown and saw them as wishful adventures. In those
days people worked on farms and visited the cities for excitement. Now people work in the cities to afford time in the
country and visit farms as a vacation. When the drudgery of
farm life permitted, leisure time was spent soaking up the
sun and swimming in the salty Mediterranean Sea. Their
favorite entertainment on the farm was the spinning of tops
on the flat ground. There would be competitions to see
whose top spun the longest. It took talent to string and un-
leash the top with a high rotation speed. Another game
involved rolling hard three-inch diameter balls against a wall
to see who could get the closest without hitting the wall. It
was very much like a game of marbles. Finally, there was the
traditional game of Bocce Ball. It is commonly known as the
Italian version of lawn bowling. These days, it is usually the
older men who are seen playing this game. The object was
to score points by rolling eight larger balls as close as
possible to the smallest ball, the 'pallina'. The person whose
ball came the closest, scored the points. Finally, if they could
get enough players, there was always a game of soccer.

In my father's youth, travel for pleasure was pretty much
unheard of. On the farm the primary form of transportation
was a bicycle. My grandfather owned the only bicycle in the
family, and it was shared amongst the family members old
enough to ride it. On those few days that my father could
get away from the farm, he would ride the narrow dirt roads
through the countryside lined with wheat fields, vineyards

and fig and olive trees. These trips were strategically planned to be taken on optimal sunny days when he would ride to nearby local villages to meet with friends. Along the way it was not uncommon to stop and chat with random villagers who would invite him in for some cheese and wine, and to discuss the latest town gossip. Italy was a very socially driven country and the townspeople loved to gather and chat the hours away. Gossip and banter seemed to be a national pastime that provided entertainment and escape from the daily drudgery of their everyday lives. Tales of spirits or ominous predictions would be bandied about and then spread through the village. Suspicious behavior became fodder for hours of speculation. Religious fantasies became fact. There was always something to talk about. And there was always something to eat and drink.

The occasional festival in a nearby town would draw in the locals. The trip into town was as much a part of the occasion as the actual event. It would take a pleasant hour-long stroll down country roads, past farms lined with wild-flowers and over the bridge to Ceprano to get to their desti-nation. The whole family would dress in their finest attire and start their trek together laughing and chattering the time away. Most towns in Italy had centralized piazzas in open areas surrounded by two story limestone and stucco buildings overlooking beautiful country scenery. The streets were cobblestone and were seldom level.

Festivals were most often organized around religious events. The parades, the eating and the drinking were designed to bring the community together. Market stalls set up in the Piazza offered trinkets, leather goods, meats, cheese, and gelato. It was always a happy time. The sound of accordions and harmonicas would fill the air. Marionettes would entertain small groups of children. Music in the square would bring everyone to their feet dancing and singing. The young children would run around in sheer exhilaration. Adolescents would seek romantic connections, carefully avoiding the watchful eyes of their ever-present family. The elderly were dressed in gray and black to signify their mourning of a lost loved one. Scarves concealed their heads as they would look on and give toothless grins as they delighted in the festival and the commotion surrounding them. Here they would catch up on community affairs, discuss the latest rumors, and pay homage to whichever saint that day was dedicated to.

My dad told me about an incident my grandfather had experienced following one of these festivals. It was late evening and my Nonno was a young man at the time. He was returning home from the festival alone on his bicycle. According to his story, he rode his bicycle along the dark country road flanked with thick bushes and trees. There were no streetlights, only moonlight. He peddled cautiously and kept a watchful eye for hazards along the way. This route was not new to him. He had made this trip many times and there was nothing to indicate that this time it would be anything out of the ordinary. Except this time, it was quite different. He was almost halfway home when a cow appeared on the road right in front of him blocking his immediate path. There was no way to avoid it. Unable to stop, he closed his eyes and waited for the inevitable collision hoping he would land on some soft ground or at least on top of the cow. Neither scenario happened. What shocked him was that he had managed to ride his bike right through the cow without coming into contact with the animal, let alone colliding. When he looked back the cow stood on the road unscathed, like nothing had happened.

The incident frightened him so much that he dropped

his bicycle and ran the rest of the way home terrified. He knew with absolute certainty how the event had unfolded. In his mind he was certain that it was not just dumb luck. He knew there were other godly forces at work. Apparently, a few weeks prior to the festival, Nonno's uncle had passed away. He was convinced that it was his uncle's spirit in the form of a cow that he had passed through. He believed in spirits and this only confirmed his beliefs. In his isolated countryside world, spirits and ghosts were believable and tales of encounters were told with amazing regularity. In hindsight, one must wonder if it was really a spirit or was it just a night of alcohol induced hallucinations. Could it have been an alibi to give him cover with Nonna for being out late? No one knows for sure, and my grandfather never deviated from his story. In the morning he went back, retrieved his bike, and returned to the fields for another day of hard work.

My father, Giovanni, or John as he is known, was the second born child and grew up with his nine siblings on that farm. There was an even split of five boys and five girls. The boys were Giovanni, Clemente, Pasquale (Pat), Silvester and Loretto. The girls were Assunta, Vittoria, Filomena, Anna, and Teresa. There were originally twelve children but sadly two had died. His sister, the first child in the family named Anna died at the age of five from an infection resulting from shrapnel that struck her in the face. It happened while on a visit to her aunt and uncle a mile down the laneway. Seemingly out of nowhere a lost grenade or landmine had detonated. A small piece of metal shrapnel lodged in her cheek and left a significant gash. Her screams were deafening as she fell to the ground crying in pain. She was quickly transported to the local makeshift hospital in Ceprano. There, after countless attempts to promote healing through medicine and family prayer she developed gangrene and died ten days later.

The family was devastated to lose such a sweet young girl. Shortly after her body was returned home for burial, the hospital was bombed. For the funeral, Nonna Maria dressed Anna in her first communion dress which gave her an angelic appearance as she lay in her little white silk lined casket. Her name was given to the next born girl in the family. This happened to be my Uncle Silvester's twin sister. Little information is known regarding the second child's death except that it was the result of sudden infant death syndrome.

As farmer's children, the boys were expected to help in the fields. My grandfather, Nonno Giuseppe, made sure he had plenty of help. Good Catholics bore many children. Dad would tell me his hard-working father was a very stern man who could easily fly off the handle into fits of rage. With that many kids to raise and a farm to tend to, one might understand why. How they managed to accomplish the monumental task of raising a large family and running a farm is short of miraculous. His short, bone-thin father sported a pencil type mustache and had dark leather tanned skin from all the time he spent outdoors working in the fields. My father and his siblings had a great deal of fear of their father. In those days, fear was an effective method of control and deterrence, especially in a family with ten children.

I experienced my grandfather's volatile temper during that visit to the farm with my mother during my early teen years. My cousin Gianfranco and I shared the upstairs bedroom in the barn. Gianfranco was born with his left arm missing past his elbow. He was the son of my father's older sister Assunta. On the main floor of the barn lived the ox and cows, while outside the chickens, goats and sheep would scurry about. Behind the barn were the rabbit cages. One day, being two energetic young boys who were suffering from boredom, we decided the bed would make a great trampoline. That is until it broke.

It was then that I bore witness to what my father had warned me about and it was then that I understood my father's fear. My grandfather slipped into a fit of rage well beyond anything my own father had ever reached or that I could have imagined. Of course, my father only had four kids in comparison to his father who had ten. So, if you prorate the intensity, you could calculate how angry my grandfather could get. Being the subject of his fit of rage, I felt my life was in imminent danger and that I would never see home again. It took only a moment to realize that we were in deep trouble. His anger was venomous as he used several common Italian cuss phrases and spoke so fast that I had no idea what he was screaming but I knew it could not be good. We hid in terror not knowing our fate. We could still hear him ranting while he dragged the bedframe down the stairs and onto the garbage pile. After some time passed, he calmed down and all was forgiven. That broken bed frame probably meant he had to buy a new one with money he did not have. That experience with my Dr. Jekyll and Mr. Hyde grandfather was forever etched into my mind. The lesson was well learned although it could have been taught without the tirade I witnessed. Never again would I jump on a bed.

Most of the time, my grandfather was not a madman. He was a very practical, likeable, and down to earth man when he had his temper under control. We had plenty of fun times with him, but we also knew that it was in our best interest to think things through before acting on some stupid idea. My grandmother, Nonna Maria was a very stout, strong willed lady. She was also kind and had a great sense of humor. Loud, passionate, and expressive, she was the stereotype of an Italian woman. She worked tirelessly day in and day out making meals and performing domestic duties for her large family. Her love and devotion for her family was displayed in every meal she cooked and in every sock she darned. Her family was her life and her reason for being.

My grandparents taught their kids to be strong and resilient. Everyone worked to support the family and the farm. Making ends meet was an endless challenge and much of what they owned was made by hand. My grandfather was somewhat of a musician and liked to hang out with his buddies from time to time and liked to go serenading in the evening. That was his stress reliever. I am not sure if my father was serious, but he would tell me that men would have a wife in one town and a girlfriend in another. Italy was very much a paternal state. Regardless of the hardships or the conditions they experienced, they managed to make a reasonably good living and have relatively happy lives.

The time that I spent in Italy as a youth was filled with the simple enjoyment of sitting around the dinner table eating, talking, and laughing well into the night. It was here that I finally got to know the family that I had only known through pictures or recounted tales. We spent hours teaching each other our native languages. These kind people never criticized my substandard linguistic skills. Rather, they told me that I spoke Italian with an English accent, making my way of speaking the language seem rather cool. My Aunt Rosa, who was married to my uncle Silvester would hold different objects and ask what it was called in English. They wanted to know because soon they were going to be immigrants themselves. They made me feel important because I was able to teach them. Most importantly, they made me feel like my presence was a source of joy and pleasure for them. My aunts and uncles were some of the most fun loving and caring relatives one could have. They were wonderful, gracious people despite the war and grueling farm life they grew up in.

Italy became a Kingdom on March 17th, 1861 during the reign of Victor Emmanuel II. The great Italian general Giuseppe Maria Garibaldi played a significant role in the 1861 Unification of Italy. Following years of growth, The Fascist movement emerged in 1919 due to Benito Mussolini who was a First World War veteran. During the years 1922 to 1943 Benito Mussolini ascended the political ranks and eventually took power where he reined with an iron fist. Prior to his alliance with Hitler, Mussolini brought Fascist law and order to a chaotic country in the grips of a depression. His methods were questionable, but for the poorer families it helped to create a tenuous illusion of security.

Some technical advances did take place at the time, but politics hampered any economic recovery. With the outbreak of World War II, Mussolini sided with Hitler and brought an unwanted war and occupation to Italy's mainland. It began the destruction of the life many Italians knew and loved. The country became divided in its loyalties. Many Italians did not want to be part of the Nazi Fascist alliance and chose to assist the allies as a resistance. In the end, Mussolini had betrayed Italy's trust and for that he paid with his life.

Hundreds of thousands of Italian soldiers with allegiance to King Emmanuel III refused to take up arms with the invading Third Reich and were imprisoned. The first signs of Italian resistance started in Naples which is about sixty miles away from Cassino. It started as an unorganized, chaotic popular rebellion after the German occupation of Naples in 1943. In other parts of the country the movement began as independent groups with a common goal. These independent groups were organized and led by previously outlawed political party members or by former resisting officers and soldiers of the Royal Italian Army. They managed to evade capture by infiltrating the German army. These groups of resistors eventually joined forces and were reorganized by the anti-fascists.

After the Allies landed in Sicily and moved north, daily life changed dramatically. The first sign of conflict was the distant thunder of cannons and bombs at Monte Cassino which served as the dividing line between northern and southern Italy. The first Monastery at Cassino dates to early 500 AD. It was invaded in late 500 AD and then reestablished in late 700 AD. It continued to be the epicenter for conflict through the centuries culminating in its most recent destruction during World War II.

The offensive on Cassino began in January of 1944 and continued until May of the same year. Men were forced to join the Fascist army, be imprisoned, or die. The Germans had taken up positions near the Abbey and this forced the allies to launch an offensive. There was harrowing combat. Dogfights would take place as war planes would fly overhead. The local inhabitants were frightened and constantly on edge not knowing the extent of the conflict and whether they would survive another day. Nights were spent wide awake ready to evacuate at a moment's notice. Their lives were filled with a constant sense of doom. The war brought hardship and famine to the countryside. It forced my father and his family to seek out alternative means of feeding themselves. With fighting all around, farming took on a higher risk for potential harm, damage, or theft of crops by invading armies and opportunists. Land mines were set in the fields by the German army. It was a risk every time my ancestors worked the land.

My father would from time-to-time recount some of the horrors of the war. I was never sure if he was able to tell the stories with such detail because he vividly remembered the terrors of the war or because he was unable to forget them. One story takes place on a spring morning after breakfast. He made the daily march to the fields with his family to tend to the growing vegetables. Even during the battles, the farm needed to function and produce. It was their only source of food and survival and it was a risk that had to be taken. They had reduced the field acreage to help avoid the risk of any potential landmines that may be set by the Germans. On this day, my father was behind the ox and plow preparing a furrow for seeds. He remembered it being a warm day in May 1944. While they scratched the soil and pulled the weeds, they heard the distant sound of combat and the familiar engine and propeller roars in the sky. It was not uncommon to hear these sounds as the war raged about forty-five miles away. They saw the daily squadron of bombers that often darkened the skies.

For some reason on that day, they stopped working in unison, stood up and gazed into the sun-soaked sky. They cupped their eyes as they followed fighter planes dodging and circling one another to gain advantage and then take rapid fire. The dogfight played out as if it were a staged event. One plane chased the other and then the pursued plane would twist and turn to avoid being shot down. One of the planes was finally hit and smoke came from the fuselage. The pilot then bailed out and his white parachute popped open. Slowly he drifted to the ground. Everyone in the field paid close attention to his path as he descended. Quickly, they ran to his aid about two hundred yards away not knowing if he were a friend or foe or even if he would be alive. My father recalled times when a parachuting pilot would be shot by the enemy as he slowly descended to earth. It was not the case this time. As soon as he landed, the pilot pulled off his jacket and ran leaving his parachute behind. He quickly disappeared into the nearby trees.

My father and his sisters ran towards the silk parachute he left behind. Out of breath, they quickly gathered it up. This was a windfall for the family. After it was collected and rolled up, they quickly headed back to the farm. Once they returned home, my grandmother started the process of cutting it into sections large enough to fashion shirts, sheets and even dresses. This was a major source of new clothing and a bright spot in a life engulfed in chaos and uncertainty. To my ancestors living through conflict near a raging war, it was a good day.

The locals would sometimes seek out a downed plane and strip it of any useful metal or parts that could be used as farm implements or currency for trading with others. Monte Cassino was only a forty-five-minute drive away and this meant that the fighting was at their doorstep. Whenever the bombing resumed it would last for several days and nights, each time reigniting fear in the locals. During my visit to the farm in the 1960s, my Uncle Silvio took me for a visit to Monte Cassino. We rode on his pale blue Vespa scooter and I was astounded by the number of war memorials that surrounded the Monastery. It just did not seem right that monuments memorializing a deadly war should surround a place of peace.

Before the Allies reached his town, the German forces held a stronghold in the region. They would set up camps nearby. It was not uncommon for the German army to round up the local men and force them to join the battle. This happened far too regularly and added to the unspoken disquiet in the region. To prevent men from being taken by the German or Fascist armies, a series of warnings were devised by the villagers. A courier would race to advise the locals of the advancing army, and the men would then know that they needed to evacuate immediately. The code phrase that alerted the locals of the impending search was "Porta Laqua" (bring the water). This would be followed by a quick exit to the hills surrounding the region where they would hide until the threat was over.

My father once calmly described an event that I found horrifying to listen to. While working alone in the fields trimming the grapevines, he could hear the distant fighting. By this time living under these conditions had become normal. He decided to head back to the farm for some lunch. Food was no longer delivered to the fields during these uncertain times. It was just not safe, and it potentially put more people at risk. As he approached their compound, his frantic sister Filomena ran to him and breathlessly told him that a warning had been issued and that he needed to flee right away. Not knowing where the rest of the men were, she assured him that he would be safe on his own. There was no time for questions, he just needed to run and save himself.

Unfortunately, his path to the hiding place in the hills was directly in the path of an approaching garrison. He had only a short time to decide his fate. Anxiously, with clenched fists and pursing his mouth, he looked around and made a quick assessment as to where the best hiding places might be. He decided the buildings would not be safe and running into the fields was filled with unknown risks. Seeing a large hay pile next to the barn, he decided that was his best option for survival. He quickly scrambled and burrowed as deep as possible into the middle of the pile while his sister carefully concealed his entry point.

Once he was hidden, his sister headed to the house as calmly as she could fearing the worst was about to happen. In the kitchen her mother was busy sewing and trying to act normal. Terrified, my father quietly waited deep in the hay-pile, as beads of sweat ran down his face. The hay was poking him making him want to push it away, but he dared not move for fear of being found. He visualized terrifying images of himself being forced to march into war. At sixteen years old he had no desire to be enlisted in a war that could end his young life. He did not want to fight for a cause that made no sense to him or for his country.

The marching garrison could be heard with its familiar terrifying boot stomp as it arrived in the small courtyard. From his position, he could hear the soldiers shuffling around the barn. He could also hear the officers questioning his sister and mother. Filomena told the German officers that all the men had run away. This did not satisfy them. They raised their voices in frustration and shouted orders to the soldiers who began a systematic search of each building. They also ventured into the bushes beyond the property sticking their bayonets into the weeds and wood piles. Finding no sign of the men angered them even more. The officer threatened my grandmother. If she was lying, she too would be taken away.

After what felt like hours, the small army seemed to give up. Dad felt relieved thinking that they would be leaving soon. Then a frightening sound pierced the silence. A couple of German soldiers started driving their bayonets into the hay-pile he was sitting in. He could feel his heart pounding.

His instinct was to run but his better judgement told him to stay put and do not move no matter what. There were several jabs into the hay. One came so close he thought it grazed his face. He was terrified but he closed his eyes, held his breath, and sat motionless. The prodding of the hay finally stopped. Unable to find any men, the soldiers left in disgust and moved on to the next farm.

After a long wait to make sure the soldiers were far away, my father crawled out sweating profusely and in near shock, but physically unharmed. He ran to his sister and his mother and hugged them. They reassured one another that it was safe now. This frightening experience raised my father's awareness of the dangers of being too far from the house. He would no longer go to the fields alone without the family knowing his whereabouts.

The typical hiding places for men were in the hillsides where the caves had been modified to house them until the danger had passed. Although it was not always possible, the men only needed minimal forewarning to reach these hiding places when the soldiers advanced. The interior of the caves had already been dug out and modified to house whole families. This modification had taken many days of labor by the locals. Candles and small fires were the only form of light that were available. During these threatening times Nonno Giuseppe would hide his sons and keep them warm with blankets that he brought back to the caves after each clandestine return to the farm. At home, Nonna Maria would have to boil pots of water over wood fires to soak the children's soiled clothes and bedding. Everyone had to wear their clothes for days on end while in hiding and this was the only way to kill the inevitable lice and bacteria. Conditions were damp, cold, and dirty, and the smell of human excrement filled the air, but this was far more appealing than the alternative of capture.

The quickly developing war also precipitated a rapid decline in commerce. Since supply routes were cut off by armies and fields were pillaged, it meant that feeding a family of twelve became a daunting task. There was a desperate need to find more sources of food than the small garden plot they now had or the few donations they received. In his desperation to feed his family, Nonno Giuseppe answered a call for cooks for the German Army. The job gave him access to small quantities of leftover food that he was able to bring home to feed the family. Occasionally a sympathetic officer would give him additional fresh food. His relationship with the occupiers helped spare the farm from complete destruction and total shutdown.

For many of the local inhabitants, days would pass where little food was available. Children cried from hunger and adults would give up their share of food to feed the young. Rationing became a way of life. Everyone had to be careful not to take more than their share just in case supplies dwindled even more. They were acutely aware that circumstances could become more dismal at any given moment. Trade and commercial operations were almost nonexistent. Businesses were shut down because no one wanted to risk their lives in such uncertain times. The most reliable source of food was anything you grew or raised. And that was only possible if it had not been taken from you by the Germans.

My father and his friends would gather to brainstorm ways to acquire needed rations. They thought about stealing from the armies. If caught, this would certainly put all their lives at risk. But in their desperation, it was a risk that this small group of young men were most certainly prepared to take. Stealing food and army rations would create a major logistics problem due to the sheer volume of food that needed to be taken. After careful consideration, stealing food from the army was bumped down to a last resort.

A more plausible option was to steal anything that could be used as a vehicle to get more supplies. This meant that whatever they found had to be easily transported or carried away. Firearms would help in the hunt for food. However, this would be a very high-risk operation and certain execution if they were caught. Civilians were slaughtered by the invaders when they would not cooperate or tried to steal food or arms. My father would say "When you are hungry you become desperate". He meant that you are willing to take any risk to feed yourself and your family. After some heart wrenching consideration this band of brothers agreed to do some nighttime surveillance to devise a plan.

My father and a small band of young men would go on recognizant missions at night to scope out the camped armies. The army encampments were set up and well organized by function. They had the camp broken down into specific areas such as latrines, sleeping quarters, mess halls and officers' accommodations. There was also the ammunition storage. This is what my dad and his marauders were looking for. In the dead of the night and from a safe distance, they would hide behind bushes and study the routines and timings of soldiers' movements. After several nights of watching and listening, they had the information they needed. They would return to their hideout and put their plan of action together. They agonized over the details and worked out methods and procedures that they thought would work. Each person had a specific responsibility, and they practiced their maneuvers until they were confident that every detail had been considered and thought out. They had to train themselves to control their anxiety and

the resulting heavy breathing which could easily be heard in
a dark and silent night. They were aware of how dangerous
this could be and they knew that they had to be extremely
careful.

Once the planning was complete and the designated
night determined, this ragtag band of amateur mercenaries
would quietly sneak over to the army base camp just a few
miles away. There they would stealthily move their way
around the armament's storage facility. They dressed in dark
clothes and charcoaled their faces. Even shiny jewelry had to
be left behind. There was no margin for error. They could
not be caught. With the utmost care and covertness, they
approached their target. They knew the operation could
take several hours and they did not want to draw any attention to themselves as they carefully crawled around the
outside of the encampment perimeter. Even their breathing
would have to be slowed down. Once they found where the
grenades were stored, they carefully started to move a
couple of boxes out of the compound. They slowly and
silently lifted each box and moved them far enough away so
they could be quickly transported without detection. Moving
without barely making a sound, they headed back to their
hideout which was nothing more than a candle lit stone
shed.

Once they thought they were safe, they opened the
wooden cases to find neatly stacked German grenades. Each
of the young men gave a sigh of relief as smiles crossed
their darkened faces. They were enormously proud of their
accomplishment and boasted to one another of their
bravery and courage. They slapped each other on the back
and popped the cork off a bottle of wine. Passing it around,
they each took a long well-earned drink. It was time to
release all that tension and anxiety by celebrating their

successful mission. Next, they split the booty evenly amongst themselves. Each boy would take his allotment of bombs and hide them in his own secret and hopefully secure hiding place for future use. What they did next with the grenades was brilliant.

These boys were not a fanciful wannabe underground counter espionage renegade force. They were simply hungry and they needed to help feed their families. The grenades would become currency for food. They were not going to be used to extort food but rather they would be used as a tool to procure food. My father's plan was to go to the Liri River not too far away, identify a promising spot and toss the activated grenade into the water. He would then wait for the blast that would launch a shower into the air with a muffled sound. This activity could only take place far from any nearby armies so as not to attract attention. He tried to do this when bombing could be heard in the distance so its sound would not be overly conspicuous. Once the river settled, schools of fish knocked unconscious or dead by the blast were floating on the surface. He did not know if it was due to the blast or the resulting shock wave from the explosion, but it worked. It was just a matter of collecting the floating fish, taking them home and dinner could be served. The surplus fish would be salted and stored for future meals. It was imperative during times of war to find opportunities that could put food on the table. This scheme was extremely dangerous but amazingly effective. However, there would only be a few missions as armies were not always in proximity. Also, as the allies moved into the area, the invaders moved out.

The Lazio region was the site of some of the heaviest fighting of the Italian campaign during World War II. Known as the Gustav Line, the Nazis held a stronghold there that lasted from January to May 1944. It was in this area that the battles of Monte Cassino and Anzio were fought before the Allies could capture the Italian capital of Rome. In the spring of 1944, after fierce fighting and countless deaths at the ongoing battle of Monte Cassino, the allies pushed the enemy forces north which ended the conflict in my father's region. An internet search for "The Battle of San Pietro" will give you a thirty five-minute Department of Defense documentary narrated by John Huston which was filmed during the allied advance in 1944. It is a visualization of how life was during that time. San Pietro was a small village outside of Monte Cassino, about thirty miles or forty-five kilometers away from my parents' hometowns.

The war left the area in ruins and somehow the inhabitants of the region would have to rebuild. Both property and lives were decimated. Many bridges had been destroyed and waterways were diverted. War equipment that suffered damage or got stuck was left behind. Civilian life became a struggle to survive and turned Italy into a nation of refugees. Families had to live in their bombed-out homes or find suitable shelter. There was extensive rebuilding after the conflict ended. Fields had to be cleared of land mines, piles of debris and damage caused by the marching armies. Replanting of crops and finding lost cattle or sheep was a daily challenge. The Allied Civil Affairs and the Red Cross played a significant role in the rebuilding of the Lazio region. Disease was a concern but fortunately did not take a foothold due to medicine that was distributed throughout the countryside. After the casualties of the war were honored and buried, neighbors worked together to rebuild homes and lives. My father and his brother spent weeks tirelessly clearing roads and reassembling homes. The rebuilding would eventually bring calm and order to the region. The town made a slow and steady recovery with shops, stores and theatres returning to help heal the wounds of war.

It would take several years after hostilities ceased and reconstruction concluded before farm life returned to some semblance of normalcy. Even so, the struggle was more acute than prior to the war. The family decided that the only way to better their lives was to branch out and seek better opportunities. With the support of his family, my father, being the oldest male was given the opportunity of his lifetime. He was about to embark on a journey to a foreign land and establish a life and livelihood that would eventually allow his siblings to follow.

On February nineteenth in 1952, at the age of twenty-four, my father boarded the M/N Vulcania in Naples. The ship was built in 1926 and became one of the largest vessels transporting passengers in the whole fleet. The Vulcania also doubled as a troop ship returning soldiers to their homes. My father bravely took that initial step to cross the ocean to North America and to what he hoped would be stability and prosperity. Family and friends gave their heart felt wishes to their pioneering voyager as he prepared to take an epic trip to lands unknown and a life uncharted. He felt both excitement and apprehension but was convinced it was the right move. The family had saved enough hard-earned money to buy his ticket to prosperity. My father's parents wept openly as he gave hugs and kisses and assured them that he would be safe and he would return someday. He promised to send money to help the family. His brothers and sisters who relied on him so dearly, wrapped their arms around him forming one big sniffling and sobbing group hug. He became a local celebrity as word spread about his impending adventure. At the docks in Naples, he waved to his loved ones as the ship pulled away and they waved back until they could no longer see it on the horizon. My father travelled on that ship with countless other young Italian men who were also seeking to build a new life.

Dad was fortunate that he had a distant relative living in America who sponsored his immigration. Once settled and after he was qualified, he too would sponsor brothers, sisters, and cousins to join him. Many Italians left their homes seeking a better life although a small percentage came to take advantage of others. This nefarious group was better known as the Mafia. Most of the legitimate hard-working Italians settled in the North Eastern United States, California and Ontario and Quebec in Canada. They came to improve their quality of life, raise families, and build a future. At the same time, they would send money back home to Italy to help their families rebuild in a poor and war beaten region destroyed by the unwanted conflict. The sad statistics are that Italy lost approximately half a million of its citizens to the war.

Immigration from Europe and particularly from Italy actually began at the turn of the twentieth century. Poverty and World War I provided two good reasons to leave a devastated, once agriculturally based country. They came to America during one of this country's most innovative and prosperous times. Industry was rapidly expanding and laborers were needed to fill the jobs and fuel the economy. The immigrants were happy to have well-paying work and to be able to provide for themselves and their families abroad. These farmers, laborers and construction workers helped develop large scale agricultural and infrastructure operations. They worked tirelessly to help build this nation that was now their new home.

Initially, some of these immigrants from European countries found life in North America difficult as prejudice, violence and unsafe work conditions hindered their prosperity. Being resilient, resourceful, and hardworking, these immigrants eventually became the backbone of progress in America. Once they were established, they also became the soul of America bringing with them many Italian customs and traditions that are shared in the cuisine, couture, and culture. My father was proud to be one of these people. Later in life, after all the years of working hard to achieve a life of comfort as a family man, my father would look at the trappings of his life with amazement and gratitude. Before he became ill, he felt blessed to be alive and living a much better life than the one he experienced back in Italy before, during, and after the war ended.

He did eventually return to Italy on several occasions. There he would reacquaint himself with those who stayed behind. Each time he returned home he would say he could no longer call Italy home. Initially his trips back to the homeland were to explore prospects of building a family vacation home. But Italy was no longer as he remembered it. The country and my father had changed, and he no longer felt the connection. He was happy to have a comfortable life in America. Whenever we complained, he would remind us that living in a war helps you appreciate what you have. He believed that anyone who experienced the true devastation of war would appreciate and respect the advantages that we take for granted. The offspring of the immigrants who came to America were raised with an ethic to work hard and achieve goals far exceeding their parents' expectations.

From the hospital window, I could see that the day was fading, as was my father. The sun was setting, and I realized that he needed to rest. We had reminisced enough for one

day. Our mental trip to Italy had emotionally exhausted me.
Our current reality became front and center once again as
my thoughts were brought back to the present. I gave him a
hug and left the hospital room so I could spend the night at
the house with Mom.

My mother was in her early sixties when Dad was diagnosed. She was strong, energetic, and totally devoted to my
father. Her dedication amplified during his illness to the
detriment of her own physical and emotional well-being.
She was stoic and the glue that held our family together.
With my father's last days approaching, we knew that it
meant she would be entering a different period in her life.
We worried that her steadfastness and the emotions that she
bottled up all these years would now be replaced with
sadness, loss, and despair. We were concerned for her well-
being once my father passed away. Hopefully, my presence
would in some small way give her the strength and comfort
that she would need to face the challenging days ahead.

10

MOM'S STORY

L eaving the hospital, I went directly to my parents' house. Mom had already prepared supper. It was one of her staple meals - spaghetti with meatballs, salad and green beans, some crusty bread, cheese, olives, and a bottle of wine. As we ate dinner and drank the wine, I told her of my day with Dad.

She asked, "How do you feel about our decision?"

The way she asked the question was surreal. The inflection of her voice dropped several octaves when she said 'decision'. There was a slight pause before she uttered the word. It was like she was having difficulty articulating it in such a way. How do you put into words that someone has decided to schedule their death for a specific day because it would be in everyone's best interest? The person you have loved and lived with for most of your life has asked you to allow them to die. There are no accurate words in the English language to describe the emotions attached to this unfathomable request.

I replied, "It is courageous. I support you and Dad in

this decision." It was difficult to utter the words with support and without emotion.

"It is best that Dad has this opportunity to decide his own fate. How are you dealing with the idea of not having him around anymore?"

She responded in a saddened tone, "We will see. I will be alone and I will miss him so much."

Her staunch Italian upbringing was kicking in. She wanted to put on a brave face. Living through the war and its aftermath of devastation and loss of life had built a hardened emotional armor around the survivors. My parents' fortitude and strength exceeded anything that those of us who have not lived through those terrible times can imagine. It is a deep-rooted coping mechanism that can sometimes be mistaken for callousness. I told her how Dad and I had talked for hours about the historical events of his life and our lives as a family. I now asked my mother if she would also share her story with me.

As we poured ourselves another glass of my father's homemade red wine, my mother looked at me and said, "I was just a young girl, maybe nine or ten years old during the war, but my older sister Amelia had some interesting experiences. Together, we can share. I will call her. She would like to hear from you."

We then called Aunt Amelia who was suffering from the early stages of dementia. Initially, she did not recognize us over the phone but it did not take long for her to realize who we were. She was eager to share her story. Her memory and recall of those bygone days were amazing and her stories were fascinating. During the years of conflict while my father was surviving on his farm, not far away my mother and her family were also coping with the struggles of war. Mom was a young girl growing up in a small hamlet called San Giovanni Incarico. San Giovanni is about seventy miles south of Rome on the side of Mounte Maurizio of the Madonna della Guardia. It dates back to late 500 BCE and has strong roots to the Lombard family. It is steeped in history and papal feuds throughout the generations. My mother had to live under the watchful eye of her mother and older sisters. My parents did not know each other during the war.

My mother, Anna Maritata, was born on Thursday April 11th, 1935 in a small village located on the side of the Mounte. Like my father, they grew up as Ciociaria, pronounced "Shushareh". This was the term given to the inhabitants that occupied Frosinone, Lazio which was between Rome and Naples. It was a term originated by the Fascists to identify the ethnic denomination. That same year, Italy attacked Ethiopia and within a year Mussolini would form an alliance with Germany. Those events would take Italy in a destructive and descending spiral.

My mother's three-story house was made in typical Italian limestone and concrete construction, situated in a condo rowhouse style neighborhood with uneven narrow cobble stone streets. Her town was built on sloped terrain. The interior of the house was painted white and had stairs leading to the upper floors where the bedrooms were located. Once inside there was a clear view from the ground floor to the third-floor ceiling. A large skylight illuminated the house. The front facade was brick and there was a balcony overlooking the street on each upper floor. The front door opened directly to the road outside. They were fortunate to have electricity in their house. On the next street there was a community fountain used for washing clothes and another fountain for drinking water. The women who typically wore long flowing dresses would walk to and from the fountain with baskets of clothes perched on their scarf covered heads. This was a common gathering place where the women exchanged stories and gossip.

On the main floor of the house, through the wooden doors off the living room, was a cantina. My grandfather, Nonno Umberto, along with Uncle Alfredo, ran a small cantina where they served deli items, meals, homemade wine and the Italian soft drink, Brio. They were also barbers. The cantina had a large wooden table with benches at one end and a serving bar with cupboards, a woodstove, and shelves of wine at the other end. Nonno Umberto would open each day at noon and serve until nightfall. This was not a nine to five business. His closing time was whenever the last patron left regardless of the hour.

My maternal grandfather was a tall overbearing but gentle man with a slight hunchback. He lived for eighty-four years. My grandmother, Nonna Vittoria, who lived to be ninety-one years old, was a short stocky lady who seemed to always be sitting on her chair in the front doorway knitting doilies or tablecloths. It gave her a view of the village and its daily activity. Her social life centered on greeting villagers as they went about their business. Conversation was the most popular form of entertainment in the village. It was not uncommon for neighbors to stop and chat for long periods of time discussing family or political events. Her workdays were spent performing domestic chores such as cleaning, washing, or preparing meals. Her daily routine would usually involve going to the open-air market to shop for that day's cuisine, picking out fresh fruits, vegetables and meat or cheese.

The men would typically take time out to have an espresso that they dipped a biscotti into at the local café and chat the time away. The café was outdoors and colorfully adorned with umbrellas advertising Cinzano or Perrone emblazoned in red, green, and white. Gentle breezes would funnel up between the rows of houses and provide a cool respite from the hot summer sun. You could hear the café owner and staff exchanging orders and briskly moving from table to table delivering their drinks and treats, occasionally stopping to share tidbits of information or just make idle but cheerful conversation with the customers.

The little village was close knit, and everyone knew each other. Similar to my father's hometown, festivals in tribute to saints were regular affairs here as well. Parades would bring the villagers out as they followed the procession up the mountain to the church for the benediction. The townsfolk would stroll the narrow winding streets past the post office, the butcher shop or police station giving a wave and a "Ciao" to the occupants. Life was generally peaceful and uneventful. The girls would study at the convent and the boys would attend school and have side jobs to help with the family finances.

My mother was the youngest in her family. She had three older sisters, Rosa, Olga, Amelia, and an older brother Alfredo. Mom also had another older brother Giovanni who contracted meningitis and passed away at the age of seven before mom was born. It was all too common in the days of struggle for a sibling to get sick and die. Coincidently, my mother lost her brother Giovanni which is the same as my father's name, and my father lost his sister Anna which happens to be my mother's name. It almost seems like they had some sort of cosmic tie and were destined to meet.

Growing up in my mother's home meant a life of strict discipline. They were taught what to do and what not to do. It was a very structured life with little freedom. Her brother Alfredo wanted to join the army shortly after the liberation, but his father did not approve of that idea. They compromised and Alfredo became a Carabinieri. He moved to Rome and became a motorcycle police officer.

As the war drew near, the peacefulness in the village ended abruptly with the German occupation. The war would have a devastating effect on my mother's sleepy little village. Like my father's farm, it began with the distant bombings. At the sound of these bombardments, some of the inhabitants would take shelter under trees. It was a futile attempt at refuge, but it was the best they could do at the time. The villagers were gripped with fear. Most of the townsfolk would flee to the mountain top with only the clothes on their back and hide in caves when the bombing got closer. When the Germans entered the village, they quickly commandeered several homes for the officers.

San Giovanni became a stronghold. One officer took a liking to my grandfather and was often seen in the cantina sharing food and wine with his officers and the locals. The family knew that they needed to find favor with the officer in order to survive and not be subjected to scrutiny and potential abuse. My Nonno Umberto and Uncle Alfredo even made repairs to the officer's uniforms. This relationship helped avoid a potentially dangerous situation.

My grandmother feared for her daughters' safety and wisely decided to keep the four girls well-hidden during the occupation. They were ferreted away to the mountain caves for three to four months after an incident that sent fear through the family. A junior officer had learned of my mother's older sister Amelia and was anxious to make her acquaintance. In one instance, the young officer approached Alfredo and badgered him to divulge the whereabouts of his sister. He refused to cooperate potentially at his own peril. The officer would arrive at the house in the evening and call out for Amelia. Each time, Nonna Vittoria would scold him and send him off until she finally had enough and alerted Nonno Umberto of the situation. Up until this point, my grandfather was oblivious to the situation as he was busy working at his business every day and night. He expressed his dismay to the ranking officer that regularly visited his cantina. To his credit, this officer then made it clear to his staff that no one was to bother the family anymore.

Life in the dark caves during this time was extremely uncomfortable but for some it was their only hope for safety and ultimately survival. There were few amenities except for those items they could haul up the mountain. A small amount of furniture, blankets, candles and reading materials were the extent of their comforts. At night it was important not to cast too much light out of fear that they would be found. Cooking was a challenge. Food would be carried to the caves in the dead of night while armies were asleep so as not to be detected. Travelling back and forth had to be done during the dark and involved secret routes concealed by brush and terrain.

After the Germans were forced out of the region, the Moroccan mercenaries or Goumiers enlisted by the French allies moved in and with that came enormous fear as they were ruthless, fierce fighters and were believed to abuse or kill young women. Their presence in the town terrified the townsfolk. When not fighting, the Moroccan soldiers would seek out women. They would use threats of physical harm just to extract information from the locals. They wanted to know where they might find beautiful young girls. When questioned on one occasion, my grandmother told the Moroccan soldiers, if you are looking for young girls go to the store and buy one. Obviously, it sounded better in Italian, but this would anger the Moroccans. Those that it did not anger would laugh her off as witless. She was being ridiculous with a purpose. She wanted them to know she did not fear them and was prepared to resist.

On another occasion one of the soldiers approached her and said, "I hear your son Alfredo has four sisters." She looked at the soldier and remarked "Four sisters? If you are looking for sisters, you should go to the convent just outside of town. There are two hundred of them there." The nuns had already made their escape well in advance. The soldier was not amused. The nuns were the lucky women. Many were not. The Moroccan soldiers were accused of committing countless assaults and rapes during this period that became a point of disputed contention between Italy and France. Several soldiers were punished for their behavior. Those who were found guilty of murder were executed.

Not long afterwards, Canadian allies entered, and the townsfolk cheered with jubilation. The soldiers were showered with adulation for freeing the village from the enemy. However, the allies' effort to enter the town and push the German army out involved endless indiscriminate bombing raids. This damaged or destroyed many homes and family sanctuaries became piles of rubble. Tanks and armored vehicles would rumble through the town to counter the attacks. The enemy would evacuate the town but take up positions nearby to avoid being easy targets. To flush them out, the allies would plan bombing missions, and this would unfortunately involve the destruction of the town. The allies and the police would do their best to forewarn the townsfolk of the impending bombing but in most cases they were only given about an hour's notice to evacuate. That notice came in the form of a siren that could be heard for miles around.

The villagers would then have to quickly gather what food and belongings they could carry in their arms and head for the protective caves on the mountain top. As the battles continued, the men did their best to search for food, foraging for nuts and whatever could be found in the woods. The younger women made daily visits to wells and springs to gather enough water for their families back in the caves. Here, life was full of fear, and difficult. Food uncertainty was always a source of tension. Searching for food in the mountains during the winter was not only difficult but dangerous if caught by the invaders. On several occasions men would leave to find water or food and would never return.

My grandmother being the tough little lady she was, refused to evacuate. Her Italian stubbornness would dumbfound the allied soldier or policeman trying to save her life. Before the bombers arrived, a soldier would check to see that the town was evacuated.

The policemen and soldiers would say to my Nonna, "Please come with us and move to the mountain. If you stay behind, you will surely die."

They would assure her that they were not trying to trick her, harm her or take advantage of her. However, she was having none of it.

She would say to them, "Why would they want to bomb an old woman like me? I don't hear any planes or bombs."

It became clear to the soldiers that they were not going to sway my grandmother. Stubbornly she stayed behind while the rest of the family evacuated and made their way to the mountain with countless other inhabitants. She must have understood engineering concepts because she would hunker down under an archway in the house during the bombings. Miraculously, she survived the ordeal even as some of the house tumbled down around her. It must have been terrifying, but her life was spared. It was not her time to leave the earth.

The final remnants of the battle at Cassino were fought in a town already reduced to rubble. After the fighting ended it was once again peaceful in the town, but the streets were hard to distinguish. The townsfolk would return and be devastated by the destruction. Screams of frustration, loud weeping and calls to God seeking relief could be heard as people gradually returned. The once lush valleys and hills dotted with olive trees were burned and destroyed. The terrain was pock-marked with large water holes left by the bombing. Skeletons of the remaining buildings protruded from the ground. Homes were reduced to piles of rubble and the ones that escaped destruction had gaping holes or craters left in them by the gun fire and bombs.

Then the monumental task of rebuilding would begin in earnest. To help with the problem of scores of homeless people, the Red Cross and Civil Affairs organized committees to assess the suitability of existing buildings. Committees designated by the community and staffed by local Italians surveyed buildings and assigned families to move into those they deemed to be structurally sound. The town had to work together to rebuild.

Looting was another problem that had to be addressed by the authorities. Goods and currency were in dire need. To make money my grandmother started selling fruit and vegetables at the train station and other locations around town. Eventually this became too daunting as she had to deal with opportunists and sometimes unsavory robbers who would steal money or food from her. The rebuilding took years and left a painful scar on the minds and souls of the villagers.

Each day during the reconstruction, men, women, and children would clamber over broken-down limestone walls and start the process of clearing away the rubble. My mother's family lived in rented accommodations during the rebuild. Her father spent months repairing the damage to their home. Unrelated families would move in together to have a roof over their heads and a warm bed. The structures that required the least repairs were rebuilt first.

American army officers took up residence next door to my mother's house. They were tasked with the rebuilding of the small village. Her father reopened his cantina and served the liberators homemade meals. As he did before with the Germans, he would once again get into their good graces by giving the soldiers haircuts and repairing their uniforms. With the army helping to rebuild the town a sense of hope was restored. Life was a struggle and had it not been for the cantina, dire poverty would have consumed my mother's family.

One by one the village homes were brought back to life. It took many years to complete the transformation and return the small village to the vibrant little town it once was. It was not until 1957 that Monte Cassino was reopened. Controversy still exists as to why it was erroneously bombed to destruction.

Now it was getting late, and my Aunt Amelia had recounted much of her experience. We bid her goodnight and hung up the phone. With that and a little of my father's fermented grape sedative in our veins, my mother decided it was time for bed. After our final sip of vino rossa, she slipped away to her bedroom with a soft, "buona notte". I moved to the living room, threw myself on the couch, turned on the television, and watched some late-night entertainment. I quickly fell asleep after what had been an emotionally and physically exhausting day.

The next morning, my mother awoke early and was brewing espresso and frying eggs and bacon. I could smell her morning wakeup call as I laid on the couch. In the kitchen, I greeted her with a kiss on the cheek. "Buongiorno Momma." We sat and quietly shared breakfast. After a coffee we cleaned up, got dressed and made our way back to the hospital to see Dad. I was eager to hear more about their lives together. We quietly drove down the country road towards town. The sky was cloudy but the air was warm as we passed the gated and well-maintained town cemetery, acutely aware that Dad was going to be resting there very soon.

11

MOM AND DAD'S STORY

Once we arrived at the hospital, we slowly walked the halls to my father's room. We passed the nurses dutifully going about their daily routine. Each one of them greeted my mother like they had been friends for life. It was obvious that she had become a cherished part of this small country hospital community which was run by a close-knit family of doctors, nurses, and aides. We continued to my father's room on the third floor.

He was visibly happy to see us when we arrived. I could only imagine the boredom he must have felt when Mom was not with him. Without my mother's company, he would lay in his bed day after day and night after night unable to move, alone except for his memories and the occasional visitor. His only friend was the television and the nurse that would check on him. He survived a whole year of hospitalization in no small part because my mother was there every day to keep his hopes up and bring him some form of joy and comfort.

Greeting him with kisses and a bit of small talk, we pulled our chairs close to his bed. We knew as we sat down that this would be one of the last times that we would be able to do so. It would be one of the last times I would ever have a conversation with my father.

I started by saying, "Dad, how about we take a walk down memory lane again today? Can you and Mom tell me your story? I know both of your stories, but I don't know your story as a couple."

I sat back and listened intently as my mother and father shared details of their experiences during their forty-eight-year marriage. Even though they did not meet until five months after their wedding, they managed to build a successful, loving relationship based on mutual respect and consideration. Even with access to the internet I do not think many couples today would be able to survive those circumstances. It seemed unfathomable how they were able to marry complete strangers, live separately and still have a successful relationship when many people are unable to do this even after living with one another prior to marriage.

I watched in awe as they recounted the story of their life together, finishing one another's sentences, embellishing one another's narrative, and sometimes playfully disputing the other's version of events. They spoke so fondly of those memories. I was proud and somewhat envious of the love they had found and nurtured. In his rough and uneducated Italian fashion my father would often say "In every marriage one person has to be the smart one and one has to be the stupid one." It was his rudimentary attempt to give words to his theory of a successful marriage. This is what I believe he was trying to say. In each marriage there are times and circumstances where one spouse must compensate for the other in areas where they lack strength, ability, or common sense. In his basic way he was an incredibly wise man. Their enduring marriage was a testament to his philosophy.

Although I remember my childhood as idyllic and free of family drama, I know my mother and father had their share of challenges during their marriage. As a child I witnessed some very tense moments when my mother had exhausted her patience with my father. The most dramatic conflict I ever observed between my parents happened one Mother's Day when Mom wanted to go out for a nice meal. My father was expecting her to prepare dinner as she did every other day of the year. My recollection of the incident was hearing my parents hurl loud accusatory words of Italian disdain towards one another. Angry words between my parents and language like that was highly unusual in our home. It was so intense that my mother packed a suitcase and insisted that Dad drive her to her sister's house. She wanted to leave immediately. That was the first time that I ever saw my father break down and cry. He was weeping. Except for the first time that I returned home from college that was the only time that I would ever see him cry. Even during his long, agonizing battle with ALS, he remained stalwart.

In a desperate effort to mediate and help diffuse the situation, I grabbed my mother's suitcase and held it tightly refusing to let it go. After a while, their emotions started to settle down. Through much coaxing, my father convinced my mother to stay and admitted that he was wrong. A détente was declared and calm was restored. I remember being so relieved. The rest of the day was quiet and subdued. Never again was the incident mentioned. And never again was Mom expected to cook her own Mother's Day dinner. Like most married couples my mother and father had their arguments, but they tried to shield their children from their personal differences.

Now as the day of my father's death approached, my

parents laughed and cried as they recalled the events that
shaped their lives and their family. Dad started off telling
their story. Shortly after his arrival in the new country he
started to work on a farm as a laborer. At first my father
worked in a greenhouse owned by the man who sponsored
him, but later he was loaned to another farmer where he
worked in apple and peach orchards as well as bean and
tomato fields as a hired hand. The farmer, Mr. Kudrock,
was a good hardworking man who owned many acres of
farmland. Farming was in my father's blood. This was a big
opportunity for my father, because not only was he compensated monetarily, but it also included a small house for him
to live in. It was a simple wooden structure located near a
barn with a small kitchen and a bed. It had running water
and an electrical outlet. The furnishings were minimal with
a small table and two chairs, and a bed in the corner. The
kitchen had an ice box and a hot plate to prepare meals. As
a single man in a strange new world, he found it exhilarating
to work hard to build his fortune and send money back to
the family in Ceprano. He felt he had finally found success.
The family back home would be so proud of him.

He toiled for two years tending to the farm, pruning
fruit trees, suckering tomato plants, spraying pesticides and
harvesting the fall crops. He learned to operate farm equipment and vehicles such as trucks and forklifts. This was a far
cry from the ox and plow he used in the fields in Italy. This
experience helped him obtain his driver's license. Until he
could afford a car, he would ride the many miles to and from
town on an old bicycle he was given. After a few paychecks,
he was able to buy himself a shotgun so he could go hunting. He would borrow Mr. Kudrock's hunting dogs, two
spaniels, and spend some of his days off creeping through
bush and forests chasing wildlife for dinner. He was no

stranger to hunting. This was a favorite sport back in Italy. He was able to do what he loved in his spare time. Since my father was an immigrant, there were not many other options for recreation or entertainment.

He learned to speak fluent English with the help of his coworkers. In exchange, he would teach them how to make wine and capicola. Dad kept a booklet where he would record words that he had taught himself. Here he would write both the Italian word and the English translation. After one long, hard day working on the farm, he returned to his house to clean up and make dinner for himself. As he approached the little shack he called home, he found a piece of mail stuffed in the door jam. He would write home regularly updating the family on his status. On occasion, he would get letters from home telling him of events back in Italy. The postage revealed it was from Italy and the return address told him it was a letter from his mother.

As he tore open the envelope, a picture fell to the floor. He reached down and picked it up. As he held it he stared for a moment. It was a picture of a pretty young girl with long dark hair and a beautiful smile. She was fashionably dressed in a head band and leaning against a railing along a body of water. She was surrounded by pigeons. He was intrigued and the image of the woman piqued his interest. He wondered if he knew her and where he had seen her before. There was a comfortable familiarity to her face. As he kept studying the woman in the picture, it finally dawned on him. Back in Italy, he had passed by her once at a hospital where they both had visited a distant relative, who by chance was related to both of their families through marriage. To be able to remember such a momentary encounter is a testament to the fact that Dad was not one to pass a beautiful girl without noticing. He wondered why his mother sent him this picture. He put the photo on his kitchen table and read the letter.

His mother brought him up to date on family affairs and the farm status. Finally, he got to the paragraph that explained the photograph. He read how, by chance, his mother had met another lady at a recent town festival and they were discussing their families. They discovered that they both had unwed offspring. In fact, my paternal grandmother, Maria, mentioned to my maternal grandmother, Vittoria, that her son was in America and he needed a wife and a family. My Nonna Vittoria was in full agreement. She suggested that her daughter Annita, who was known as Anna would be a wonderful wife for Maria's son, Giovanni, better known as John. In the letter Nonna Maria asked her son how he would feel about marrying this beautiful girl. My father had some serious thinking to do.

He was soon consumed with thoughts of marrying this woman but he did not give his answer immediately. He thought about it for days and laid in his bed at night imagining the possibilities. It took a bit of time, but finally he decided that she would make an ideal wife. She was young, good looking and Italian. What more could a man want? The fact that she was living close to his family back in Italy was also a good thing. The chance encounter between the mothers had to be some type of omen. This match was meant to be.

By this time, my father had made friends with other Italian immigrants. His next oldest brother Pat had joined him in America a few months prior to this time. His friends and his brother overwhelmingly supported this decision and encouraged him to act on it. He was now twenty-six years old and alone with no romantic possibilities. In the old country, this was a good age to be married and start having kids. There was no reason why this should not be the same in America.

He made a final decision. He would notify his family that he would marry Annita Maritata. That evening, he wrote the letter that would forever change his life and set my life in motion. He placed his acceptance letter in an envelope, put a stamp on it, rode his bike to the post office and dropped it into the mailbox. There was no turning back now. At that moment, my fate and the future of my family was sealed in an airmail letter. It was not long after, that events were set in motion to make this marriage actually happen. There was only one problem. He was in America and she was in Italy as were both of their families. This was going to create a logistical and financial problem. It was one that would require a considerable amount of thought and innovation.

It was now the summer of 1953 and Dad was consumed with thoughts of marriage. After the excitement of the proposal settled down, he had some serious problems to deal with. He had made his proposal by mail and now the reality of making it happen weighed on him. It became clear to him that he could not afford to go back to Italy, get married and then come back with his new bride. He had to find a solution to his marriage dilemma. Preparations had to be made and events and venues had to be scheduled. The church, the priest, the invitation, the venue, and the caterers all had to be dealt with and money was scarce. San Giovanni, my mother's town, was a buzz with the matrimonial details. Everything was set as the wedding day approached except for one detail. The groom could not attend. It would be financially impossible. The only solution at that time was marriage by proxy. This was a legal form of arranged marriage in Italy. Sight unseen except by photo, two people who never formally met were going to commit to one another until death do they part.

My eighteen-year-old mother grew more anxious as the wedding day approached. She was filled with excitement and anticipation, as was her mother, who worked hard to make all the arrangements a reality. Time was of the essence. The day of the wedding was a cool but beautiful winter day, and my mother was beaming with joy in her bright white wedding dress. It was Sunday, December 27th, 1953. An event such as this did not go unnoticed in the small village. On the other side of the ocean the groom was in farm clothes bailing hay. It was not exactly how you would visualize your wedding; however, this was not a normal wedding.

My dad's father arrived at the ceremony in a tuxedo looking quite debonair, as his duty was to stand in for his son at the wedding. The church ceremony high on the mountain top was followed by a celebration in the village below. The long two mile walk from the church to the celebration attracted much attention. It all went off without a hitch. The party was like any other wedding celebration. It was filled with laughter, joy, food, and lots of wine. Hundred's attended arriving on bicycles, horses or on foot. The only noticeable exception was that the groom was not in attendance. Unable to be present at his own wedding, Dad gathered his friends and relatives together after work and they held their own modest celebration an ocean away.

My mother and father would have to wait another five months before they would be together and meet for the first time. It would be twenty-five years before they shared a celebration of their marriage when the family arranged a surprise anniversary party for them. It would be a total of forty years from their original wedding before my mother

and father would renew their vows in a special church ceremony. Finally, they would have a celebration of their union
with their children and other family members present. This
time they were both able to attend and were able to say their
vows to one another for the first time.

Now that my father was married, in addition to the
money he sent back to his family in Italy, he also sent money
to his new bride for English lessons. The plan was that my
mother would learn to speak English while still in Italy.
Unfortunately, the lessons did not help her. Learning to
speak conversational English was trial and error and was not
taught effectively in Italy. While they waited to be together,
there were no long phone calls, no Facetime, and no emails.
There were, however, letters that went back and forth over
the ocean as they put their thoughts and their dreams into
words, imagining life together even though they knew little
about one another. They would try to describe their
everyday lives and activities through pen and paper. My
mother found it hard to comprehend my father's occupation
which he described as working in large houses made of
glass. He told her these buildings were called greenhouses.
She could not wrap her mind around a glass building that
housed cucumber plants. Farmers grew tomatoes and
cucumbers in these greenhouses? Why were they not grown
in the fields? It was a concept that was foreign to my mother.
Nights were spent longing to meet as they repeatedly read
and reread the letters. Through the power of words on
paper, they developed a love and devotion for one another. It
was the kind of romantic love that grows from reading
letters again and again from a sweetheart. Stories were
exchanged and my father would explain to my mother how
much better life would be once she came to America.

Throughout this waiting period, my mother would stay

at my father's farm living with his family and sharing a room with his younger sister, who was my mother's age. This was a harrowing experience for her. Moving from a village to a farm had its challenges but it gave her some perspective on my father's life. There she would learn what farm life entailed and learned to perform light chores. It was an opportunity to understand what her new husband's life and family was like. Being a village girl, she experienced severe culture shock. Chores filled the day and nights were spent dining and chatting. It was a life she had never before experienced but she knew that this was what her life would be like once she arrived in America.

She would spend weekends back at her own home in San Giovanni to catch up and remember what the finer trappings of village life felt like. During this period, her travel arrangements to America were being prepared. She needed a health clearance. She also applied for her passport and visa. As the cool winter gave way to the warmer spring days, my mother's sailing date grew closer and closer. Her anxiety also grew with each passing day. Soon she would be taking an epic voyage by herself. She had grown up in a protective bubble surrounded by family, so the prospect of sailing to America was both exciting and frightening. Her mother and father were sad to see her go but were excited for the new life she would have. Her village held a goodbye party to celebrate her new adventure and to wish her well. Her brother and her sisters were emotional. They were sad to see her leave but happy that she had an exciting new life ahead of her with her husband.

My mother boarded the SS Constitution in Naples on Saturday May 1st, 1954. She was nineteen years old as she waved goodbye to her cheering family. The SS Constitution was an American ocean liner commissioned in 1951 that sailed the Genoa, Naples, Gibraltar, and New York route. Later in its history, the ship would gain celebrity status. It was featured in an episode of I Love Lucy, and Grace Kelly travelled on it in 1956. The following year Cary Grant was filmed aboard the ship. Many years later, scenes were shot using the Constitution in shows such as Magnum P.I. and Naked City.

The ship's next stop was Genoa and then it would be onto Ellis Island in New York. During the stop in Genoa, my mother met her older sister Rosa and her husband who were living there. He was a member of the Italian navy, so they were given permission to board the ship. Sharing an espresso and discussing her impending adventure helped pass the time. She could get off the ship with them and stay portside until the purser called for boarding. Her sister then handed her a farewell bouquet of flowers to take on her voyage. The last picture of my mother in Italy was taken in Genoa. She stood on the dock next to her ship in full makeup wearing a beautiful outfit and holding a bouquet of white lilies. They hugged and held each other tight, gave each other the traditional two cheek kiss and tearfully bid "arreviderchi, buon viagio, Ciao Bella, ti amo". They did not know when or if they would ever see one another again.

The Atlantic crossing was not a tropical cruise for Mom. Nine days in rough seas made her appreciate *La terra fermi*. She was seasick the entire journey and remained holed up in her cabin. This was her first time on a ship and the rolling waves that rocked the boat made her sick. She could barely move. The crew and fellow passengers treated this young girl well and her fellow travelers would check on her regularly. During this period, she could barely eat and what she did ingest, she was unable to keep down. A bit of fresh air helped occasionally, but for the most part it was a voyage of misery. She cried continuously and longed to go back home to familiar San Giovanni even though she knew that going back was no longer an option. There was no future in San Giovanni. She was betrothed and, on her journey, to meet her new husband and to see her new home.

Finally, after nine long sleepless days and nights at sea, on Monday, May 10th, 1954, the majestic Statue of Liberty broke the horizon bringing exuberance and cheers to the weary travelers. She had missed her Mother's Day arrival by one day. At last, she could put her foot on land once again. As the ship docked, she peered out of a porthole window to see what awaited her. Ellis Island was teaming with activity. It was incredibly busy with crowds of immigrants dashing around searching for family. Looking both ways through her tiny window, she strained to see if there were any familiar faces waiting for her on the dock. She had made prior arrangements to meet some family members on arrival, but she did not see anyone familiar.

After wiping her eyes, checking herself in the mirror and taking a deep breath, she carefully gathered up her worldly belongings, joined the flow of anxious travelers and slowly followed the monstrous crowd to the exit ramp. Once she disembarked, she expected to be met by three cousins who had planned to travel from Massachusetts to New York to meet her. Unfortunately, the ship had experienced some delay crossing the ocean and had arrived a day late. Her cousins were not there to greet her because they had to be at work the following day.

This left her alone once again and unable to communicate effectively. She knew little English except for what she was able to learn from the lessons back in Italy. She felt abandoned and unclear as to her next move. Panic was setting in. Before leaving Ellis Island, her cousins had wisely alerted a customs agent who happened to be Italian to look out for their cousin. They told him what ship she would be disembarking and asked him to take care of her. With a bit of good fortune and an extremely helpful man, the Italian speaking customs agent took her under his wing and found her a spot to sit and wait. He was clear with his instructions. He told her not to move and not to speak to anyone. He said he would return shortly.

As she sat waiting, she could hear ear piercing chatter from the thousands of arrivals scrambling to get into the long lines to get their clearance to enter the country. After the customs officer returned, he checked her passport and saw that a phone number had been scribbled on a scrap of paper stapled to a page in the passport. He made the call and contacted Mr. Kudrock, my father's employer. The officer told him he would make sure Annita would board a train to his town, but he needed confirmation that Mr. Kudrock would be there to pick her up. Otherwise, she would be placed back on the ship and returned to Italy. He gave the officer his assurance that he would be there. She was off to her next adventure. The following two days would be spent on a train that would finally take her to her awaiting husband.

Once she boarded the train, it became evident that two days on the train was not much better than the boat ride. The only bright spot was that she was homesick but thankfully not seasick anymore. She was offered a cabin with three other travelers. Fear and anxiety forced her to gracefully decline. She took up a position on a padded seat. She lived and slept on that chair for the entire trip, crying most of the way. Loneliness and fear were her only emotions. To make matters worse, the train travelled through a bitter snowstorm in upstate New York. Annita had never seen that much snow before. Looking out the window, she thought she must be in the Arctic. She was sure she was headed for a life amongst the Inuit. Maybe the glass houses her new husband described were igloos. When the train pulled into the station at her destination, the weather had improved considerably. There, to meet her were four gentlemen, one who claimed to be her husband. She studied his features and shook her head.

"No," she said in Italian, "My husband has a scar over his right eye." She then pointed out my father. They all had a good laugh and started greeting one another in Italian.

This was not a romantic 'miss you so much' encounter like in the movies even though this was the first time they would meet face to face. This first encounter was very formal even though they had developed affection for one another through mail. It was a bit awkward but congenial with friendly hugs and kisses. Mr. Kudrock was the owner of the car that was driven to the train station. As they drove the forty-five minutes back to their nuptial home, discussions about life back in the old country were shared. Mom was still somewhat apprehensive and physically exhausted after her long journey. She tried to adapt to her new environment and to her greeters. This was all very foreign to her. She was a young girl in a far-off land meeting people she had never met before and they were all men. Once they were delivered to their matrimonial home, the newlyweds were finally alone.

Now it was time to get to know one another better. Mom went to her room and slowly unpacked still feeling very insecure and alone. She had left her family and everything that was familiar behind in Italy to start a new, committed life with a man she had never met. This was an awkward and challenging way to marry. When you consider all the obstacles a relationship faces today during a time of instant communication, it is remarkable that two people could marry sight unseen living an ocean apart. Today my mother would be referred to as a mail order bride. Back then it was a typical immigrant story. That they were able to succeed in life, make the marriage last and continue to love and be devoted to one another until my father's dying day fills me with awe. It is a testament to the type of people my parents were.

Once she finished her story, I reminded my mother of a recent trip I had taken to New York City. I told her about some research I did at the Public Library. There I found passenger lists showing names and dates of Italian immigrants. I also found evidence of a plane trip Dad had made to New York City back in the 1960s. It was likely a stopover on his way to Italy, but it was fascinating to see my father's history memorialized in print. I told her I had made a point of visiting the Statue of Liberty so I could envision her landing in America.

She was quiet for a moment and then said, "Oh yes, I remember the Lady. When we made it to America and our stop was Ellis Island, I got a good look at her. After that horrible bedridden crossing, it was a marvelous site to see. I have never forgotten her."

The 'Lady' was proposed by Frenchman Edouard de Laboulaye as a monument for the United States in 1865. The sculptor Frederic Auguste Bartholdi designed it to commemorate the centennial of the American Declaration of Independence in 1876. American workers built the pedestal, and the French delivered and assembled the Statue. In 1892, Ellis Island opened as an immigration station. It served in that capacity for more than sixty years until it closed in November 1954. This was shortly after my mother's arrival. Ellis Island saw more than twelve million newly arrived immigrants pass through its doors. Over four and a half million of those immigrants were Italians. Today those Italians represent one fifth of the United States population. Immigration to a nation is usually prompted by the lure of hope and the freedom to pursue opportunity and happiness. That is what makes a governed country great. Many immigrants like my parents arrived filled with that hope, and many of them were able to fulfill those dreams.

While my mother was preparing to travel to America, my father found a suitable nuptial home where he and his bride could begin their life as husband and wife. He settled on a second-floor apartment on the main street in the downtown area of that small factory town. The rent was reasonable and it had two bedrooms located above a small general store. You could step from the second story window onto the roof of the adjacent building. There my father strung a clothesline to hang the wash. The street below was outside the front windows. The furniture was second hand and minimal. The kitchen table and four chairs were made of wood painted white. The table had two hinged leaves to make it larger when guests visited. Cooking was done on a wood burning stove. There was a radio and a used couch with some small tables. The apartment was sparsely decorated but it was luxurious compared to my father's shack on the farm, and it was definitely a step up on the ladder to success.

It was not long before my mother was homesick for Italy once again. For the first few weeks my mother and father did not share the same bed because they wanted to get to know each other much better. Mom's homesickness had her crying almost every day wanting to return to Italy. Dad had to replace his tough macho demeanor with compassion. This helped my mother cope and helped her ease into her new way of life.

The cold temperatures and deep snow during the long dark winter months did not help with the adjustment. She was not used to this kind of weather. It is not often that Italy experiences snow. Here in her new home, winters would be cold and would last half the year. Thankfully, kindness and friendship came through the landlord's sympathetic wife, who gave Mom a set of yellow Corelle dishes as a welcoming present. She loved those dishes and gave them special status. She hated to use them. The kind woman also helped my mother with her English. Those were moments when my mother felt more at ease and she started to feel like she belonged.

As time passed, she slowly adjusted to her new world and became much more connected to Dad. To make life more enjoyable, they began to socialize with other Italians. It gave the women an opportunity to dress in their fancy long flowing dresses, high heels, and bright red lipstick when they went out to dance at the local community hall. Not to be outdone, the men wore their best suit, tie, and shoes. To entertain themselves at home, they would invite friends and family over to the apartment for wine and games of Scopa, an Italian card game that was played like euchre except that every card was a type of face card. There were no numbered cards. Over time, her new friendships, her new past-times and most importantly her new husband began to feel normal and her life in Italy became more and more a memory of days past. She still missed her family back home, but she was totally immersed in her exciting new life in America.

Being the youngest girl in the family back in San Giovanni, my mother did not have to learn the culinary arts.

Her mother and older sisters took care of all the family meals back home. Mom would say she did not know how to boil an egg, let alone a noodle. The task of cooking initially fell on my father's shoulders but with time my mother's cooking abilities improved and surpassed Dad's skills when she added her own special touches. She took pride in her culinary creations and felt a sense of accomplishment and happiness when it brought a smile to her husband's face.

Once she settled into her new life, it was not long before I became a twinkle in my parents' eyes, and I joined the ranks of baby boomers. Baby boomer is a term used to describe those of us who were born between 1946 and 1964. Boomers make up a substantial portion of the world's inhabitants and about twenty percent of the American population. In effect, I became my parents' post-war effort.

They lived in that cramped apartment for a couple of years after I was born. While my parents worked, my Aunt Vittoria, who was my dad's sister, became my caregiver. My aunt was the most fun a little kid could ask for. I was dropped off at her house in the early morning hours where I would spend time with my two cousins, Bruno, and Aldo. I thought of Aunt Vittoria as my funny aunt. She had a hilarious sense of humor and she could make the most mundane event fun. She has always been one of my favorite relatives. She seemed to be eternally happy and always spoke loudly with a level of excitement. Nothing was boring to her. Her favorite cuss was "vaffuncula" with a dose of "Che Cazzo or Come see va - capisci". This was usually followed by raising her hand and saluting. She liked to recount what she calls Bobby's money story. One day after she came in from hanging laundry on the clothesline, she caught me pulling paper money out of her purse and flushing it down the toilet. She frantically stuck her hand down the toilet to retrieve the money but it was long gone. She would add that I did not even use it to wipe. What a waste!

My mother told me that as a four-year-old child I went missing from our home on Martin Drive. My parents were going about their daily routine oblivious to my whereabouts. Like most parents of that time, it eventually dawned on them that they had not seen me for a while. Not too concerned, they searched each room in the house. After finding no sign of me they instantly blamed one another for losing me. By this time both of my parents were in a total panic rushing about the neighborhood searching backyards and yelling my name up and down the street. When they returned to the house the phone was ringing. Mom was sobbing as she answered. On the other end my Aunt Vittoria calmly asked if they were missing anybody. After the initial joy that I was safe, my mother cried once again because she was so relieved. I was returned to them and given a clear order never to do that again. I had made the half mile walk from our home along sidewalks and across an intersection to my aunt's house. I believe it was that event that heralded the beginning of my lifelong love of adventure and discovery.

During the early days of their marriage, more of my parents' brothers and sisters were sponsored to make the journey to America. They were part of the large economic migration that occurred after the war. This was a class of migrants who typically emigrated from their homeland in search of a more economically stable country. They were seeking an improved standard of living by escaping the poorer conditions and lack of job opportunities in their original region. The United Nations refers to them as migrant workers.

North America was experiencing a post war surge of

economic activity and invited immigrants to fill the new job opportunities brought on by prosperity. Many of these jobs were in farming or industry. My father sponsored three of his brothers and sisters and my mother's older sister. Some of their cousins came over as well creating a small family dynasty in their farm town. After finding simple, inexpensive homes to rent and eventually buy, they took jobs in farming, packing and food processing. Some were able to get funding from established relatives to buy their own farms, become citizens and build small income producing ventures of their own.

With so much family living nearby, we were always having gatherings. As more children were born, the size of the get-togethers grew. My father had the only car in the early days and would become the designated driver for all the relatives, taking them to appointments and any other important meetings they needed to attend. At any time of day or night my father would get calls to hurry over and drive an expectant relative to the hospital. Since he had the only car in the entire extended family it was also his duty to be the stork. One time when he helped his pregnant sister into the hospital, a doctor asked him how many wives he had since he had already driven several pregnant women there. Finally, when my mother was the one in labor, he made sure that the doctor knew this woman was his actual wife. Back then men were not allowed in the delivery room nor did they want to be. Childbirth was relegated to the doctors, nurses, and the expectant mother. But he would always be pacing in the hallway until the little bundle of joy arrived. He was devoted to his entire family.

After living in that tiny apartment, we moved to the bigger house on Martin Drive. By this time, my father had a steady job and could get a mortgage. It was solely his responsibility to make a living, put a roof over his growing family's head, put clothes on their backs and feed them. Initially, my mother's job was to tend to the home and the children. Mom and Dad taught us to do the right thing, to respect our elders, to be tough in difficult times, not to be afraid to work hard and not to expect life to be easy. We also learned that it was alright to take a break and enjoy the beauty and joy that a good life could offer.

My father applied for and landed a job at the food processing factory and most nights came home from his shift with boxes and cans of unsellable products. It was called D and R, meaning the cans were dented or had a bit of rust on the outside. The company would sell these to the employees at deeply discounted prices. Canned spaghetti or beans became one of my favorite meals. Eventually my mother found seasonal work outside of the home. She held various jobs at the tobacco factory, the canning factory, and the fish plant. She even picked strawberries for twenty cents a pint.

Initially Dad harbored that Italian macho mindset that his wife should not work and that she should be home taking care of the house and the kids. This attitude did not pass muster with Mom. The women's rights movement was silently picking up momentum even in immigrant homes in small towns. Many spirited debates ensued. It only lasted for a short while because Mom finally put her foot down and insisted that she was going to get a job. She assured my father that she could both maintain the home and earn a paycheck. My Aunt Vittoria entered the picture when my father wanted to know who would watch the kids while she worked. She became our caregiver when our mother was not at home.

Dad was an AFL-CIO union member and would come

home evenings frustrated by events he witnessed at work. He felt there were workers at the plant that did not pull their fair share. He felt they were taking advantage of the protection the union gave them. He was not exceedingly popular with the less than fully productive guys because he would warn them "if you don't put in a good day's work, one day this plant will shut down." They laughed and told him that would never happen, saying "the company needs this plant." My dad's prophecy eventually did come true but he would not see that day because he passed away before it happened. He was one of the lucky ones who retired with a pension before the decline and eventual closing of that plant. The pension provided a comfortable life during retirement, and an income for my mother after he passed.

We were a typical Italian family, eating endless amounts of pasta, meatballs and insalata. My father, having extensive farming experience, would buy live chickens and rabbits. Not knowing his motives, we would feed them and make them our pets. Unfortunately, my father had other plans for our 'pets' and they would eventually appear on the dinner table. We would watch in horror as he chopped a chicken's head off in the back yard where it would run around the yard as blood squirted from its neck in a headless frenzy. My father would laugh as we stood wide eyed and stunned. This was normal at my father's farm in Italy where survival was more important than sentiment, but to us kids it was horrifying.

My father convinced me that I should learn to play the accordion as was the tradition for young Italian offspring. Although we lived in America, this would cement my Italian heritage and make the family back home proud. I complied with his wishes and attended weekly lessons with my junior accordion. He loved the sound that the accordion made.

When it came time to graduate to a full-sized instrument, he was prepared to have one shipped from Italy. That was when I had to be honest and tell him I did not want to play anymore. I wanted to play the guitar. He was heartbroken and my music lessons ended. I realized years later that his father played the accordion and that is likely what motivated him to have an accordion player in the family. There are times I wish I had stuck with it and fulfilled his dream. Despite putting down the accordion, I never did learn to play the guitar.

Quite often, we sat around the old three-foot-high waterfall wood grained radio and listened to the scratchy reception of the local broadcast. Dad loved to play his vinyl records on the console Hi Fi stereo that was so big and so beautifully finished it could double as a casket. I developed an appreciation for older Italian songs like 'Al di la' and artists like Jerry Vale, Dean Martin and Frank Sinatra as well as bands like the Tijuana Brass. Today, that old waterfall radio sits in my mancave.

Evenings were spent in front of the old picture tube television. We loved watching weekly series and the occasional special program. The television stations in our area broadcast family favorites like The Beverly Hillbillies, Lawrence Welk, Red Skelton, Perry Como, Daniel Boone, or Davey Crockett. While still in pajamas we huddled around the television on Saturday mornings watching Bugs Bunny or Road Runner. After school it was Gilligan's Island or Leave it to Beaver. We watched old RKO movies starring celebrities like Tyron Power or Sophia Loren. The Mitch Miller Show was an anticipated Christmas time event along with roasting chestnuts or 'castagne' in the oven on a baking sheet or peeling persimmons and eating them

If a war movie happened to be on one of the four channels that we had access to, my father always settled in and watched it intently. He would narrate some of the action and highlight episodes that hit an emotional note with him. I would notice tears building up in his eyes during some of the war scenes. I would avoid making eye contact with him at those moments as I did not know how to handle it. I was too young to understand the impact that the war had on my father and the permanent scars that it had left on his psyche. The Second World War took one of his sisters and turned his peaceful world upside down. As an adult, I now know it was the painful memories that brought my father to tears. As a young child, it was bewildering to see my otherwise strong, seemly invincible father emotionally crumble watching a movie. Hearing their stories was enriching, but it was time to go.

The Time Draws Near

And now the day had passed, and we had reached the end of our visiting hours. Dad was tiring, it was getting late, I needed to get back to my house and Mom needed to get home. I needed to prepare for my Monday morning routine back at the construction site. Mom and I kissed Dad's forehead and expressed our love for him, and then we quietly turned and left the room feeling downhearted. We made our way back to my truck. I drove my mother home so I could start the long trip back to my house knowing that I would have to repeat this journey the following weekend. The only difference was that the next time I came to town it would not be to spend hours talking with my father. It would be the day my father's life would end, and my life without him would begin.

The drive back home was spent rehashing all the events that had just taken place. I was oblivious to the soft jazz playing in the background as my thoughts consumed me. I doubled back through my hometown past the hospital and as I approached the downtown area, I slowed down to view the shops and stores that I had once patronized. The old Woolworth's was now a carpet store. There used to be an A&P grocery store directly across the street. I can remember shopping with Dad when twenty dollars would get you three or four large paper bags of groceries, long before plastic bags became the norm. Then I passed the old Diana Sweets restaurant where we would stop after school or on the weekend for a plate of French fries and gravy. It had now been repurposed into a lady's wear shop. And Toni's barber shop was not Toni's anymore.

Around the corner I could see the old sporting goods store. Many weekends were spent bringing our slot cars to the enormous track on the second floor above the store. Each car was a mirror image of the racer's imagination. The power plant on the course had a tiny electric motor that was fed a full twelve volts of electricity through the bushes that contacted the copper strips on the track. A hand-held controller governed the amount of power that could be sent to your track. We were able to race four cars at a time. The weekend remote-control slot car races where these mini stock cars would barrel down the straights at high speeds and slowdown in time to take the tight curves were eagerly anticipated. The curves were deadly. A race was usually lost after a car took the curve too fast. The inevitable end over end crash and subsequent tumble off the table would bring the competition to an end. Days spent racing our cars would pass quickly.

As I continued my slow drive, I stopped for the red light at the four corners. I recall in the mid sixty's when fire destroyed one half of the four corners. My eyes wandered up to the second floor of the corner bank building. There, my Uncle Silvio, and I had assembled three flights of scaffolding so we could repair the brickwork on the upper wall and parapet. From that vantage point, I used to watch the daily activities of people going about their commercial affairs. That was the last job I held in my little town. I had just graduated from college and my uncle put me to work in his fledgling concrete and brick laying company. It was during that time, a friend and classmate named Peter called to inform me of a job opening at the engineering company where he worked. Manual labor ended abruptly that day. I left town to pursue my chosen career as an engineering and construction planner in a small city that would eventually become my new home.

A few store fronts down the street I could see where my father and I opened my very first bank account. The bank was now a stationary store. On the left-hand side of the street, I could see that the Vogue Theater still operated. As a child, Saturday afternoons, were often spent eating popcorn and chewing twizzles as we watched the latest cinema release. During the Christmas holidays my father would drop a bunch of us off at the Vogue to meet Santa Claus. That jolly white bearded man in the red suit would hand us candy canes. I have so many fond memories of time spent at the theatre. It was comforting to see that it was still intact and still operating.

The light turned green and I took my foot off the brake and lightly pressed the accelerator to continue my slow drive through the tiny town. Next, I passed the second story apartment where Mom and Dad began their lives together. It was where I was conceived. I looked up and smiled. In my mind, I imagined seeing my nineteen-year-old mother looking out the window of that second-floor apartment and waving goodbye as I drove past. I glanced into the rear-view mirror and watched the town fade away as if it were a distant memory. As familiar as the old town was, it was not the same at all. Time had moved on, and the place that I once knew as home was strangely unfamiliar. I understood in those moments of nostalgia what they meant when they say that you can never go home again.

It was extremely late by the time I pulled into the garage at my home. The weekend had left me mentally and emotionally exhausted and I could not wait to curl up and get a good night's sleep. When I awoke the next morning, I slipped on my running gear and ran a few miles up the river road, showered, dressed, and drove to work. There I immersed myself in my usual Monday morning project related activities. Keeping busy kept me from thinking about the upcoming weekend.

My week was consumed with phone calls, meetings, inspections and pouring over drawings and plans. I had six coordinators who helped direct traffic on the site, which proved immensely helpful as my thoughts often wandered to my father. I wondered what Dad must be feeling and thinking at that moment. Was it fear or was he relieved knowing he would not have to continue in this agonizing state? I thought about how different life will be for my family without our father, my mother's husband, and our family patriarch. As the week slowly ticked down to Saturday, I found myself thinking more and more about the upcoming weekend and the finality of what was coming. It was almost incomprehensible to think that I would be going home so my father could die.

The entire family was now aware that my father was going to take that final step to end his life on Saturday. We were all consumed with grief and sadness. Early in the week, Hilda flew in to be with Dad, Paula, Joe, and Mom.

They took turns spending time with Dad. They shed oceans of tears as time ticked down to the weekend. Relatives were calling Mom to express their sorrow and tried to give her strength through words of support. As much as they tried, there was really nothing that they could say or do to alleviate the grief. They visited Dad and spent time with him recalling happier days and a life well lived. We were all trying to bring some sort of closure to an incredibly sad time. None of us were ready to let Dad go, but we knew we had to honor his wishes. We knew that it was not a decision that was made lightly. In his own selfless way, I think he believed that this final act would not only relieve his suffering, but it would also allow us to move on with our lives. He always put his family first and he was taking care of us to the very end.

Finally, Thursday arrived, and I left work early to make that drive back to see my father. After work that afternoon, I once again headed to my childhood home. It was an unusually sunny day and under normal circumstances, it would have been a pleasant day for a long drive. However, that was not the case that day. I played music to distract myself, but I could not focus. Random thoughts raced through my head. I just could not fathom what life would be like after this weekend, without my father. He was such a huge presence in my life in so many ways and it was just unfathomable to think that he would be gone.

I thought about the funeral arrangements we had already made years ago when we thought we were going to lose him. Thinking that death was imminent, the funeral home was notified, and all the preparations had been set. Mom had settled on a burial versus the traditional mausoleum. She had dutifully picked out plots for herself and Dad along with a headstone. One side of the stone would read *Giovanni Battista*, with a picture of Dad that she had chosen. The other side of the stone would read *Anna Maritata*, with a placeholder for her picture. I was grateful that a photo was yet to be chosen. Back in Italy, burials took up a considerable amount of land and gravesites were a scarce commodity. Interment in a mausoleum was the preferred form of burial. The term mausoleum was coined during the Greek antiquity after the death of the Ruler Mausolus. The tomb of Mausolus was the origin of the term mausoleum. Many years following my father's passing, I would return to Italy with Uncle Alfredo and visit the mausoleum of my mother's parents and the farm where my father grew up.

Today's drive was uneventful and passed quickly. I arrived at my parents' house early in the evening where Mom, Joe, Hilda, and Paula were all having dinner. When I walked in, they stood up to greet me. The sorrow in the room was palpable. Rather than the joyous welcome of times that now seemed from bygone days, I could see the sadness in their eyes when they hugged me. Although this was not a happy reunion we managed to raise one another's spirits by our mere presence. I sat down for dinner with them as Mom filled my plate with pasta and poured me a glass of wine. We talked about happier times with dad and reassured mom we would get through this as a family. We wanted our mother to know we would be there for her as long as we all lived.

The following day was spent with Dad, keeping him company, and trying not to show any signs of despair or hopelessness. It was meant to be a time for family, a time for peace and a final time for togetherness. As the afternoon turned into evening, we headed back to the house. After dinner, I felt the need to spend one last night with Dad.

Hilda felt the same way. Paula and Joe had their families to attend to, so we gave one another a hug and said good night to them as they headed home. Hilda and I drove to the hospital and made our way to the room where Dad was resting quietly. Since visiting hours had ended, we had to ask for permission to spend this last night with our father. The nurses were sympathetic and obliged. We pulled softly cushioned chairs into his room and then leaned over and told him we would not leave him this night. He was able to acknowledge us with his eyes. We sat with him throughout the night and listened to the pumps and various beeping sounds as the lines bounced up and down on the small medical displays. It was quiet and the lights were dim throughout the hospital.

My sister and I would engage in idle conversation as the nurses performed their duties. Watching them scurry up and down the hallway, we realized what heroes the devoted nurses were. During this long night we saw firsthand that my father was not the only patient receiving their devoted and attentive care. They worked diligently and seemingly tirelessly comforting numerous patients and administering medication. Without fail, my father would cough about every thirty to forty minutes as his phlegm obstructed the breathing equipment. Each time an alarm would be set off. And each time a nurse would rush in and clear his airways. She would pause for a few minutes to ensure he was comfortable and then quietly leave.

By spending the night in his hospital room, I was able to see what Dad's life had been degraded to. Although I am not a spiritual person, I felt that my need to be at my father's bedside one last time was actually someone guiding me back. By seeing firsthand what his nights were like, I was better able to understand his decision and find peace with it.

It was at this point that I saw how terribly difficult his life had become. He was lucky to get a complete hour of sleep. Up until this point I had only been with him during the day engaging in upbeat conversation. I was overwhelmed at my father's courage to make the decision to end his life. He knew the time had come to end his journey. This was no longer a life. It was merely existing.

We tried to get comfortable and close our eyes, but the chairs were not designed for sleep. My father's breathing alarms also kept us awake. Our comfort and sleep really did not matter. We just wanted to share as much time with him as possible while he was still with us. Even though he was in and out of sleep, merely being near him brought us comfort.

With the dawn came a flurry of activity. The halls filled with doctors, nurses, patients and loved ones. The hospital seemed to come back to life. My sister and I awoke from our brief sleep and moved closer to Dad. I doubt that he had managed to get any rest. He was awake and still had intravenous tubes and air hoses connected to him. The nurse came in and pulled off his mask and cleared his tracheostomy so he could talk to us. I was so consumed by the night's events, that to this day I cannot remember much of our conversation. The trauma of the night left my sister and me profoundly emotional. With tears slipping down our faces, we told Dad how much we loved him and how much we would miss him.

Soon after, my mother entered the room. We hugged one another and wept. The rest of the family began to arrive. Within the hour, all the relatives were sniffling and weeping in the hall outside his room. I recognized the voices and left the room to greet them and thanked them for coming. In groups of two, they slowly entered my father's room and spoke to him as they sobbed. They would clutch his hand, kiss his forehead, and wish him peace. They too would tell him how much they were going to miss him. He laid in his bed holding back emotion, being the backbone of the family right to the end. Gracefully, he thanked each one and even in this moment he tried to make them feel special with some antidote of information that they shared over the years. They thanked him for coming to this country and planting the seeds that grew into this magnificent family. All of my aunts, uncles and cousins got a chance to say good-bye. They waited outside the room as the designated hour approached. My mother, sisters and brother and I sat with my father saying anything we could to keep ourselves from sinking into despair. My mother and father shared some moments of humor that distracted us. We did anything we could to keep us from thinking about what laid ahead of us.

It was then that my father's youngest brother, Uncle Loretto arrived and waited in the hall. My mother noticed him at the door and with a bit of anxiousness alerted my father to his brother's arrival. Still maintaining his sense of humor even at this dire time, my father called out "I'll be out there in a minute" which made us all chuckle. His brother entered the room in tears and hugged him. He was too choked up to say anything. The whole scene felt surreal. This could not really be happening. Maybe this was a dream. The precious time we had left was quickly coming to an end.

The doctor arrived and checked my father's vitals. He turned to us and said only the immediate family was allowed in the room. He then explained what was going to take place so we would be prepared to deal with the upcoming events. Truth be told, there was nothing the doctor could say to prepare us, but it was a kind attempt. I had spent almost fifty years with this man. For the last three years, I watched this disease progressively debilitate him. For the past week I had been preparing myself for this moment and yet I was not at all prepared. I believe there are some moments in life that nothing can prepare you for. You just have to experience it and find some way to come to terms with it later.

The anesthesiologist entered and began inspecting my father's breathing equipment. Afterwards, the doctor returned closing the door behind him. We all wept openly and said our final goodbyes while clutching his hands. His arms were no more than skin on bones. Vivaldi's 'Four Seasons - Winter' was playing in my head. I thought of all the seasons of my father's life and realized that there was not a season for what was to come. The doctor motioned to the anesthesiologist who slowly turned the breathing equipment off. The doctor administered medication with a syringe to ease any pain. We watched and listened as my father's breathing became shallower. His eyes slowly shut, and he drifted away. His tired and battered body was shutting down. He took a final gulp of air and then fell into a relaxed and motionless state. We were all still holding onto him. My mother held one hand and my father's oldest brother held his other hand as life slowly slipped away. My siblings and I were at his feet holding on to him.

After about fifteen minutes, the doctor said, "He has passed."

It all happened so quickly.

The doctor said, "You can stay with him as long as you like." He took my mother's hand and continued, "You are an angel and the reason John lasted as long has he did." He then gave us all a reassuring touch and quietly left the room so we could spend our last moments with Dad in privacy. Mom held Dad's hand tightly with tears in her eyes and spoke to him as if he were still alive. Her words were the final goodbye. "John, we had an exceptionally good life together and we raised a good family. Your suffering has ended, and you can now rest knowing that we will be alright. I tried to save you but I could not. We will see you again one day. Love you."

After a while, I slowly stood up, said my final goodbye to Dad and numbly walked out of the room where our relatives were hugging my mother as she wept. As I walked away wiping my eyes, I turned and took one last look at my father lying on the bed motionless. Through the blur of tears, I felt thankful that he was finally at peace and free of his broken body.

12

GOODBYE DAD

The next time we would see Dad's body was at the funeral home. Our extended family had gathered to pay their final respects. His brothers and sisters all came with their children to say goodbye. My mother, myself and my siblings lined up to greet the visitors as they passed by and gave us hugs and words of support before crumbling into tears and sobs. Each mourner would touch and then kiss my father's forehead. The kiss is symbolic of one's respect for the deceased.

My oldest daughter Erica made the long journey to be with me. She rushed to my side and sobbed as she clung to me. As the last of the mourners moved past the casket, we moved closer to Dad. The curtains were drawn so we could spend some private time together. We were armed with some of my father's favorite things. Much like the practice of old Egyptian burials and in the customary Italian tradition we carefully placed a handheld ham radio, some jewelry, a bottle of wine and some small personal artifacts into the casket next to his body. There is an Italian belief that if you send the dead away with their most cherished belongings they will not return to earth as a ghost or spirit. My mother kept his wedding ring, and I was given one of his other cherished rings. I still wear this ring every day.

When the curtains opened once again, we noticed more people had arrived. Friends from my father's past and five nurses in their scrubs were lined up at the back of the room. The funeral director gave a small sermon and then the casket was moved to the waiting hearse to be taken to the church. We would carry the casket into the church, place it by the alter and then take our places in the pews. It was raining that day for the first time in weeks. Dad said he was mad as hell he had to leave so he would make it rain. He was always a man of his word.

The priest, dressed in his dark robes, flanked by his white robed assistants gave the funeral rites. We all sat and listened intently. Following his sermon, it was my turn at the podium, and I gave my last tribute to my father. As I delivered the eulogy, I could hear sniffling and sobbing and it took all the strength I had to stay composed. These were the words that I shared with our family and loved ones.

Before I deliver this eulogy, in keeping with my father's wishes there will be no luncheon after the funeral.

Today I want to leave all of you with a lasting memory of my father. For many of you these words will not be new because many of you knew him well.

From the moment I could understand who this man was I discovered that my father was totally committed to his family, my mother, my brother, and my sisters. He was dedicated to his trusted friends.

He worked hard at everything he started, giving 110% of his time and effort. He was never a quitter. He believed in honesty, integrity, dignity, and respect.

My father never touched us as children. We just knew when he spoke, he meant it. So, we did our best to stay out of trouble.

He loved his family, his friends, and his life. He believed in honor and that your word was your guarantee. He was a self-made man. My father would rather build it himself than give in and buy it. To this day I still catch myself thinking — you know I could make that.

I watched him make his first carbon arc welding machine, build an assortment of electronic gadgets, build the house we still live in, make the wine we drank and grow the food we ate.

I believe Thomas Edison, Henry Ford and Alexander Graham Bell would have saved themselves a lot of time if they had my father working for them. They probably would have had time to invent even more things.

As the eldest son in his family, he protected and helped raise nine young brothers and sisters on an old farm back in Italy. He was the frontiersman who carved out the trail for his brothers and sisters to come to this great country of ours.

My dad knew how to live and have fun too. He and my mom enjoyed many family gatherings, laughing and spending countless hours just being together, kibitzing with old friends and making new friends wherever he went. He accepted everyone. His love for his children especially could be seen in his eyes and in his smile. He was always the teacher.

Often, we would sit up nights over several bottles of wine discussing everything from the latest events to life and death itself. He loved discussion and would taunt you to frustration just to keep the discussion going. Once you caught onto his little gimmick the discussions would take on a more lighthearted tone.

I believe all his questions about life and death have now been answered.

My father loved to travel and see new things and new places. When he couldn't get out, he would bring the world into his home through the programs he liked to watch, the music he played and through his ham radio where he developed a worldwide friendship. His radio was his window to the world community. Talking to his network of radio colleagues injected new life into his tired and weak body. Though he had never met many of them he cared for them like he had known them all their lives.

His love had no boundaries. My father portrayed a strength and toughness, but we all knew deep down inside he had a soft heart and gentle soul.

My brother and sisters learned a lot from him. We have much to take with us. He taught me to be a man. I know he passed these gifts on to each and every one of you who were fortunate enough to know this wonderful man of strength and honor.

His courage and bravery saw him through his final moments when he decided his work here was completed and that his almighty Father needed him to come home. He probably needed to fix a car or something.

In any case we will miss you dearly, Dad. You've been an inspiration and you've touched our hearts.

John, Dad, Grandpa, Nonno, Papa and trusted friend we love you and you will always be in our hearts. Thank you for all that you were and all that you gave us. Ciao Papa, Buon Viaggo, Ti amo.

In closing, I want to thank everyone who graciously helped my father and mother and family, these past three years. Thank you to the doctors and the hospital staff who were like family and friends and especially to my mother for being Dad's guardian. May God Bless All of You. Thank You.

Following the church service, the funeral procession made its way through town escorted by police through each intersection the entire five miles to the grave site. By that time, the rain had stopped, and the sun was peeking through the clouds. As we passed oncoming traffic, cars would pull over to pay their respects. At the grave site, the partly cloudy sky was accompanied with a bit of a chill. We quietly and slowly gathered for final prayers and the lowering of the casket. Each one of us in attendance took turns walking past and throwing a flower or a handful of the piled dirt onto the lowered casket.

My father insisted that there should be no gathering after his funeral. He made that clear prior to his passing and in keeping with his wishes we complied. He felt there was no reason to have a party after a person dies. For him, it was a time for mourning. I cannot say I was in full agreement because it does give the surviving family an opportunity to relive happier times and share their sorrow.

Shortly after the funeral my mother insisted on removing all evidence of Dad's medical equipment from the house. She did not want to be reminded of his illness. She wanted to remember him as the vital man she married, not the struggling, gravely ill person he was in his final years. As stalwart as she was during the illness, the past few years had traumatized my mother more than any of us realized. Her brave façade hid her anguish and pain from us. I collected, cleaned, and sanitized all the breathing and medical equipment and delivered them to the hospital as a donation. His wheelchair and exercise equipment were donated to a local charity.

For two years following Dad's death, Mom found it difficult to cope with the loss and loneliness. Collectively, we kept a close eye on her. My sister Hilda and I would call her each week and my sister Paula and brother Joe who lived close by would visit her regularly. My mother's sister Amelia and Amelia's in-laws routinely visited to keep her company and build her spirits up. She became a hermit and was lost now that her purpose was in question. Days and nights would slip by, one after another, week after week. The weeks turned into months and eventually into years. With the passage of time and the support of her family, she was slowly able to emerge from that darkness. Sorrow only heals when you give yourself permission to heal.

Eventually, she would drive to see her sister and even began dating. She started to attend dances with a female neighbor who became her trusted friend. We could see the excitement of life taking ahold of my mother once again. From the age of eighteen, she had played the role of the Italian wife and mother. It was a role she cherished. Loving her husband and family, and successfully raising four children was her purpose in life. She often says that she would not change anything in life except having more time to share with my father. She adorns the house with Dad's pictures and she insists that he watches over all of us. Mom makes regular visits to Dad's resting place where their carved head stone sits, knowing that one day they will be together again. She makes sure that his gravesite is free of leaves and weeds and that the headstone is pristine. Even in death, my mother takes care of the man that she loved and lived with most of her life. Even though the loss of her husband profoundly altered her life, in some ways nothing changed at all.

13

FINAL THOUGHTS

When my parents embarked on their separate journeys to America, I am sure they could not have imagined the beautiful life that was to lay before them. They were among the millions of immigrants that left their homelands in Europe, Asia, and Africa, expecting to initially struggle while learning the language and achieving financial stability, but hoping to eventually find love, create a family and build a life in their new home. These immigrants came with barely enough money to survive one day and yet somehow achieved huge results through determination and hard work. They came with various skill sets and helped build the infrastructure of the nation.

Work and life were difficult, and sometimes in the more dangerous lines of employment it could be tragic, but they held on to the belief that a better life laid ahead. They were willing to take the risk. They struggled for years, only able to meet their basic needs. Undeterred, they saw their current difficulties as a necessary stepping-stone to a better life. They knew that hard work was the key to ending hardship. What they lacked in money and resources they compensated with an over-abundance of faith and hope. And like thousands of other immigrants of the time, they contributed to the American culture with their traditions and cuisine. I was once told the impact of immigrants from various countries on the American way of life, was like cooking a good pot of minestrone soup. One culture was the legume, one was the vegetable, one was the spice and another was the broth. Each ingredient was necessary to enhance and compliment the flavor of all the other ingredients. Together they blended to form a perfectly seasoned pot of minestrone soup.

These Italians never forgot their origins but were still loyal and faithful to their new nation. The basic values of hard work, respect and love of family and God were ingrained in them and subsequent generations of children. This second generation was commonly referred to as Old School because they were raised in their parents' images but with an expectation to achieve even more success than their parents. They were expected to go on to higher education and often became leaders in the community, industry, and country. My parents' goal when they arrived in America was to be able to feed and clothe themselves and their family and have a better life than they had in Italy. The goals that were laid out for me were centered on self-awareness and finding emotional fulfillment through my endeavors. The immigrant dream for their children had evolved from merely satisfying rudimentary physiological needs at the bottom of Maslow's hierarchy of needs pyramid, to also achieving psychological and spiritual stability. This transition produced mature, methodical members of society grounded in faith and love of family.

My parents achieved their American dream. Along with my sisters and my brother, I am the realization and the endgame of my parents' goals. They lived a comfortable life rich in tradition, love, family, and religion. They never gave up their Italian culture and found a way to live it within American society. I do not think they ever could have imagined how many lives they would change and influence throughout their lives together. They dreamed big and they achieved even bigger. And yet, they remained humble in their lifestyle and in their attitude. They had nothing to prove to anyone and were always there with advice and help for everyone. They gave the best of themselves to their children and led by example. Family always came first. They were the sun, and we orbited around them.

When my father retired, he planned to finally enjoy the life he had built without the daily obligation of an eight-hour shift. My parents planned to travel and hoped to spend more time with one another and with their children and grandchildren. They just wanted to sit back and relax knowing that everyone was alright. What none of us anticipated was ALS and the brutality of the illness. It is still not a clearly understood affliction and it struck our family with devastating consequences. My parents' work ethic and determination could not produce anticipated results this time and spare them from this brutal debilitating disease. The cruelty of ALS is that it not only alters the lives of those who are afflicted but it emotionally and physically alters the lives of their families by delivering gut-wrenching hardships. As families struggle to provide support and care for their loved one, they lose sight of taking care of themselves. They sacrifice their own lives and compromise their health in a hopeless effort to care for their beloved family member.

My father's journey gave us an acute awareness and appreciation of how health care workers bravely deal with life and death every day. Today they risk their lives to fight novel viruses that spread with a vengeance. There are no adequate words to express my gratitude for these often unrecognized and under-appreciated caregivers. They do not perform a job; they fulfill a calling.

As our population grows so do the number of those afflicted with ALS. After my father's death, we learned that the man who bought and moved into our Martin Drive home had also succumbed to the disease. Could environment be a factor, and could my father's illness be connected to that house that is the source of so many happy memories? As a family touched by ALS, we are forever connected to the disease and help in small ways such as donating to the cause. Research is ongoing as we await a breakthrough to combat this crippling ailment. We wear t-shirts adorned with my father's picture when we get together to celebrate his life or walk miles in his honor at ALS walkathons.

As unbearable as my father's death was, life has continued to move forward for my mother, my siblings and myself. My mother has grown to be an older version of that nineteen-year-old that stepped onto a ship in Naples back in 1954. Her life is now filled with happy memories and a large family with grandchildren. All the eight-millimeter home movies that my father left us have been preserved. From time to time, we take out the old projector and watch our family's happy memories. It allows us to relive the days when life was simple, when we were young, and when my father was still with us.

Mom continues to enjoy cooking and is devoted to her children and grandchildren. She is proud of our accomplishments. The grape vines that my father planted still grow outside the back door. I have come to see my parents' journey through life as an odyssey. They overcame so many obstacles and still persevered and never gave up hope until there was no hope to be had. It was then that the bravery that brought them to this country once again kicked in.

They taught us that regardless of ethnic origin, race, or religion everyone leaves a footprint in the world and leaves a legacy for their descendants. The legacy may be the garden or the plant that your father tended to or the special meal that your mother lovingly made. Most often the legacy is intangible. Long after your parents are gone, who they were, what they did and what they taught, lives on in you. Each generation will build on it and pass it on to subsequent generations. Each one of us creates our own unique place in the world and memories of our life linger long after we are gone. My father's legacy will be the bravery that it took to come to this country and his determination to build a better life. His love of his family and new country was ingrained in all of us. Even though he no longer walks this earth with us, he is still a part of us, and we can still feel his presence and his love.

Even now, this indominable family carries on each year when we get together at the annual family picnic or at a Christmas party. We still eat, drink, and laugh as we enjoy one another's company and recount our family history over and over again. And we always pay homage to my father who began the pilgrimage to this country. The family continues to grow as the younger generation continue to better themselves by entering higher education in law, science, medicine, and politics. And every subsequent generation continues to make the previous generation proud.

ACKNOWLEDGMENTS

The effort to chronicle these stories required the help of my extended family and many friends and associates. The list begins with my father and mother, and my aunts and uncles who shared their stories and played a leading role in my life and in my book. Without their help to reproduce tales of days gone by this book would not have been possible. My dear wife Donna and close friend Martha David helped with the editing. My siblings' encouragement fueled my desire to preserve my family's story. I would also like to thank Sabrina Flynn for her literary experience and guidance. A special recognition goes to my loving Aunt Amelia who, while struggling with dementia, retained total recall of her life in her quaint village in Italy while a devastating war raged through it.

ABOUT THE AUTHOR

Robert lives in South Carolina, the Palmetto state, with his wife Donna and their cat Clipper. He studied Project Management at Ryerson University in Toronto, Canada and had a long career in heavy industrial construction that took him around the world. Consulting, coaching, and mentoring occupy his time now along with him and Donna's other loves - family, travelling, art, sailing, motorcycling, kayaking and music.